'The inhabitants will have the satisfaction of value of the land created by themselve benefit'.

Too much had to be raised in bank loans, on which interest was payable immediately. So for many years the financial situation of First Garden City was precarious and development slow.

The Cheap Cottages Exhibition gave a stimulus to the construction of factory workers' housing, the need for which rose with the arrival of the first two substantial companies in the town in 1905, Garden City Press and Healy Gresham Engineering. A company, Garden City Tenants Ltd, was set up in the same year with the aim of building affordable cottages. It managed to erect over 300 before the First World War. These cost, on average, about £150 to build, and rents were between 5s 6d and 6s 6d per week (27½p to 32½p). First Garden City Limited also established its own subsidiary for the same purpose, Letchworth Cottages and Buildings Ltd. The third principal builder was the Howard Cottage Society, formed in 1911. Between them, they built 1,060 small houses before the First World War.

After the 1909 Housing Act made it easier for local authorities to build houses, Hitchin RDC built some 100 homes – its first four cottages cost a total of £560 (£140 each) and were let at 4s 6d (22½p) a week.

With the 1919 Housing Act requiring local government to take the initiative in the provision of adequate housing, the new urban district council set about the development of Pixmore Way and Jackmans Place and 707 more houses went up under the 1919 Act. Another Housing Act in 1923 resulted in a further 226 houses – by now costing over £400 each to build, with rents at between 7s 3d and 13s 6d (36p-67p) a week.

Most subsequent developments up to the 1960s were predominately council built. In the case of the Grange Estate, there was a serious argument between the UDC and the company over compulsory purchase of the land. Only since the 1970s has the majority of construction been once again privately sponsored.

Growth was much slower than envisaged. The population rose about 5,000 every 10 years to 1971 and then flattened off; the planned population of 32,000 was not reached until the 1991 census. These are the population figures together with the main road and housing developments that were in development at the time:

Letchworth Population Growth

1901	566	In Letchworth, Norton and Willian villages
1911	5324	Cheap cottage areas, Spring Road and Campers Estate, Birds Hill, Ridge Road and Pixmore Estate, Common View, Sollershotts, Norton Way
1921	10,802	Rushby Mead, Pixmore Avenue, Common View, West View
1931	14,454	Bedford Road area
1941	21,968	Estimate (total enhanced by evacuees)
1951	20,322	Grange Estate
1961	25,511	Jackmans Estate
1971	30,945	Lordship Farm Estate
1981	31,559	
1991	32,099	
2001	32,932	

This is far slower than achieved by more recent planned towns such as Stevenage, designated a New Town in 1948.

The Battle for Letchworth

The company finally managed to break even in 1911 and made £3,812 profit in 1912. A dividend of 1 per cent was paid in 1913 and, with a suspension of dividends during the First World War, the full 5 per cent was reached in 1923, with a backlog in dividend payments at 5 per cent of £133,245. The company continued to turn in small but steady profits, reaching £25,929 net in 1939. By 1935 the

The Grange Estate, London County Council overspill housing built at the start of the 1950s, was the first major post-war development in Letchworth. It was designed by Courtenay Crickmer.

whole of the £300,000 share capital had been taken up by investors, and in 1937 a start was made on repaying to shareholders the accumulated dividend.

Meanwhile, Howard's principle of applying the unearned increment in land values to the wider benefit of the community had been picked up by central government. In his 1909 Budget, David Lloyd George, then Chancellor of the Exchequer, introduced plans to tax the 'natural' increase in land values – the unearned increment. The company protested, and Lloyd George gave assurances that he would not apply taxation to the Garden City. But the principle had been established.

After the Second World War the new Labour government's 1947 Town and Country Planning Act in effect nationalised development values in all land – in a logical extension of Howard's principle, it sought that all such enhanced value should be held in common by the state. In theory, First Garden City, as a private company, could be taxed at 100 per cent on this increment. At the same time, as a direct result of the case for garden cities made by Howard – who had died in 1928 – and his followers, the government planned a number of new towns to receive overspill population from London and other big cities, to be built by Development Corporations that would in due course hand over their assets to the local authority. In this way, the government would keep overall control of developments while preventing excess profits falling into the hands of builders and developers.

Astonishingly, First Garden City made no representations while the Town and Country Planning Bill was at consultation stage. The Urban District Council, however, met Lewis Silkin, minister for town and country planning, to argue that Letchworth should become a designated New Town, as had already been decided for Welwyn Garden City, managed by a Development Corporation. The memorandum creating the Welwyn Garden City Corporation had stated: 'The Minister…thinks it undesirable that a private company, however public-spirited, should, by virtue of its ownership of most of the land and buildings, be in a position to determine the character of a whole town and the living conditions of the majority of its inhabitants. Such power…should be vested … in a body representing the people.'

The meeting between the council and the minister stirred the company to protest and they met the minister themselves on June 9 1948, at which they agreed to act like a Development Corporation in that, once the plan for Letchworth was complete, they would dispose of their assets to the council. Having received these assurances, Mr Silkin agreed to leave Letchworth alone.

The Crisis of 1960-63

It was then that the company started to desert its original principles. At an extraordinary General Meeting on September 15 1949, its Memorandum of Association was altered to provide that, when the company was wound up, any surplus would be distributed to the shareholders. Originally, only 10 per cent was to go to shareholders, the remainder to the town. The company argued that since the development value had been nationalised, there would be no benefit to the town in any case. In the ensuing argument with the council (which was itself a shareholder) the company did, however, acknowledge its moral duty to the town and agreed to the setting up of a 'Common Good Fund' to support community projects. This proposal was implemented and the Common Good Fund crept upwards year by year to £14,000 by 1961. Meanwhile First Garden City's profits grew steadily, to £24,702 in 1954-5, the year in which the then Conservative government reversed its predecessor's policy on land development values, giving the company control again of its unearned increment.

The result was that First Garden City, for the first time, had the status of any commercial property developer. Its chairman, Sir Eric Macfadyen, pledged that the company had a moral obligation to the town and would therefore not engage in profiteering.

But the company was publicly quoted on the stock market. Its shares started to rise, and dividends were steadily increased.

In 1960, First Garden City became the subject of a takeover battle, first from a property developer called Raglan Group Property Trust and then by Hotel York, a holding company owned by Mrs Amy Rose, who professed her intention to create a family trust. On December 1, former UDC Chairman Ernest Gardiner, supported by many of the original pioneers, including Charles Purdom and Frederic Osborn, called a meeting to 'Save the Garden City'. The UDC had already recognised that, even if Raglan or Hotel York could be fended off, it would only be a matter of time before a larger predator came along. Advised by the area's Conservative MP Martin Maddan, it began to formulate a private parliamentary bill to retain the unearned increment for the town rather than see it be passed to private landlords. The town clerk, Horace Plinston, was instructed to work with parliamentary advisers to draft the legislation.

On December 15, Hotel York gained control. Amy Rose, its chairman, became managing director and her son Michael gained a seat on the board. After the company's annual meeting on February 16, she succeeded Ralph Edge as chairman. Within a few months the company started selling three freehold plots, allegedly to test the market.

The Council's private bill meanwhile was moving ahead, receiving substantial support in both houses of parliament, not least from Lewis Silkin, now Lord Silkin.

The company resisted, but retreated during the bill's committee stages until eventually the argument centred on the amount of compensation the company would accept. Purdom comments in his account: 'The argument that there was an inherent right to do what one pleased with what had become legally one's own could not be sustained against history, long practice, public interest and what was in the end shown to be the requirements of mere business honesty.'

The bill passed its second reading in the Commons on March 20 1962 by 246 votes to 13. Its second reading in the Lords on June 28 was unopposed and Royal Assent was achieved on August 1, with the vesting date set for January 1 1963.

The New Era

Under the Letchworth Garden City Act, a publicly appointed Letchworth Garden City Corporation took over the running of the town estate. Three of its board's five members were nominated by the Minister of Housing and Local Government, with one each from the County and Urban District Councils. Plinston, one of the architects of the arrangement, defended this indirect democracy on the grounds that politics should as far as possible be kept out of the Corporation.

There remained the major hurdle of compensation to the shareholders. Following lengthy haggling between the Council's opening offer of £2,650,000 and the Company's demand for £3,718,582, a midway figure of £3,115,000 was reached at the end of July 1966, a sum that could have imposed a heavy burden on ratepayers. However, by this time the estate was generating respectable profits, and it was paid off by mid-1968.

By the mid 1970s, when it was generating annual profits of £300,000 and more, the Corporation was at last able to start to fulfil Howard's project by ploughing back money into the town's facilities. Apart from many small organisations that benefited from grants, such as youth clubs, sports clubs and facilities for the elderly, there were five major projects involving substantial capital expenditure: the Ernest Gardiner Day Hospital, the Leisure Centre, Standalone Farm, the Garden City Heritage Museum and a community hall, Plinston Hall. All these form significant landmarks and, with the possible exception of the Leisure Centre, are institutions unlikely to be provided by local authorities for other similar sized towns.

Relations between the Corporation and the local authority were, on the whole, somewhat less fraught than during the 1940s and 1950s, particularly since the Urban District Council became subsumed into the North Hertfordshire District Council from April 1 1974. Though based in Letchworth, the new council had a much wider remit than the old, encompassing the market towns of Hitchin, Baldock and Royston and villages in an arc round Stevenage. One of its early acts was to designate a large part of the centre of Letchworth a conservation area under the Civil Amenities Act of 1967 to preserve the best of the architecture and open spaces.

While the two bodies – Corporation and council – had distinct powers, there was also therefore a potential overlap, with both playing a planning and conservation role. For residents it was not always clear which did what, or why. The Corporation's remit was limited to the land it owned, which meant that two large areas, the Grange and Jackmans estates, owned outright by the urban district council, fell outside its province and remain beyond the authority of the Corporation's successor, the Garden City Heritage Foundation.

4. ARTS AND CRAFTS
Architecture in Letchworth

Much early Letchworth housing style is 'Arts and Crafts' – the name given to the movement led by the designer William Morris and artists of the Pre-Raphaelite school such as Dante Gabriel Rossetti and Sir Edward Burne-Jones. The Arts and Crafts movement believed that much of traditional England had been lost in the regimented terraces of the cities. In earlier ages, people had lived in cottages that were not mass produced or jerrybuilt, and in towns and villages that had grown in an unplanned, organic manner. In Morris's somewhat romanticised view of old England: 'There was a sympathy between the works of man and the land they were made for. It is neither prison, nor palace, but a decent home.' So Arts and Crafts practitioners often sought to revive older styles of building, including features such as half timbering, oak doors and Tudor style chimneys.

'Letchworth Vernacular'

We can look at pictures of early Letchworth houses and streets, with people posing in Edwardian costume. The houses we can relate to and recognise straight away; it is the Edwardian fashions to which our eye has to adjust. Except for some of the details of the features and fittings, we would be quite happy to build houses like these today.

This demonstrates the success of the Arts and Crafts style of building, as interpreted by the town's architects and builders. They had developed what Miller and other professionals call a 'vernacular' style – a style suited to the place and almost timeless. The early builders looked around the area and copied the local styles, particularly the local materials of brick and plaster rendering, and used tiles rather than slates for the roofs.

Letchworth Architects

Consultant architects for First Garden City Limited were two second cousins and brothers-in-law, originally based in Buxton, Derbyshire, BARRY PARKER (1867-1947) and RAYMOND UNWIN (1863-1940). Both firmly believed that archi-

Icknield Way takes its name from an ancient track and has many interesting houses, including Cheap Cottage Exhibition entries.

South Place, at the junction of South View and Sollershott East, designed by Courtenay Crickmer in 1911.

tecture had a social purpose, and Unwin in particular had grown up in Morris's socialist movement and been a friend of the socialist philosopher and 'simple lifer' Edward Carpenter. His background was in the design of industrial housing in the Derbyshire coalfield. He spoke at the Bournville conference that established the Garden Cities Association, and in 1901 he and Parker set out their views on architecture in their key work, *The Art of Building a Home.*

Once appointed to the Letchworth project, they moved first to Baldock and then Letchworth, into new offices that now form the Garden City Heritage Museum. It was from there that the first planned town was directed.

After Letchworth, Unwin went on to work on Hampstead Garden Suburb, where he had an office from 1906 onwards. He gained further fame by writing a polemic, *Nothing Gained by Overcrowding*, to propagate the policy of low density housing, and later played a key role in the design of social housing, becoming first Chief Architect and then Chief Technical Officer for Building and Town Planning for the Ministry of Health, which had responsibility for housing in the 1920s. He was president of the Royal Institute of British Architects in 1931-3 and knighted in 1932.

Parker, who lived in Letchworth for the rest of his life – his home was alongside the office – continued to design many Letchworth buildings, particularly the Broadway area in the 1920s. President of the Town Planning Institute in 1929-30, his biggest project outside Letchworth was the Garden Suburb of Wythenshawe, Manchester, from 1927 onwards.

Arriving from Buxton as part of the Parker and Unwin team, before branching out on their own, were ROBERT BENNETT (1878-1956) and WILSON BIDWELL (1877-1944). These were among the most prolific of Letchworth housing designers, doing work for the cheap cottages exhibition, the Howard Cottage Society, and, after the First World War, the Jackmans Place development. Many of the town centre shops are their work. Bennett and Bidwell built fine houses for themselves, Bidwell living at 7 Willian Way and Bennett eventually moving to Hall Barn, The Glade, in 1923.

COURTENAY CRICKMER (1879-1971) also built his own house in Letchworth (15 Baldock Road, one half of a semi-detached pair) in 1905 and stayed for the rest of his long career. His housing is found all over Letchworth, from workers' housing in Norton, to the Urban Cottages in Lytton Avenue, to progressively larger houses in south Letchworth, and finally the Grange Estate which he helped to design in the 1940s. Of his public buildings, the most prominent is the library of 1937.

CECIL HIGNETT (1879-1960) was also a protégé of Parker and Unwin. While

Building materials and styles varied enormously. This example of timber boarding is in Icknield Way.

Details were made to count, as this window design in an early Garden City house shows.

34

he too designed a number of fine and varied houses, Hignett is perhaps best known for his factories, the Spirella Building being his masterpiece. Another, now sadly demolished, was the British Tabulating Machine factory in Icknield Way, a fine art deco building, although Irving Airchute in Icknield Way is still there for comparison. His house in Letchworth was Three Gables in Croft Lane, one of the few thatched buildings in the town.

The doyen of the Arts and Crafts architects was M H BAILLIE SCOTT (1865-1945) who, though responsible for only five houses in Letchworth, strongly influenced others. It was Baillie Scott who led the medieval revival, using exposed beams, open plan halls to enlarge the living spaces, Tudor style arched doorways and chimneys, plain wood crafted doors and floors, bay window seats, and hand crafted fittings such as iron hinges and latches. His Elmwood Cottages (7-7A Norton Way North), though too expensive to qualify for the Cheap Cottages Exhibition, attracted enthusiastic reviews for their revival of the country cottage feel.

Other fine Letchworth houses are by HAROLD CLAPHAM LANDER (1868-1955), ALLEN FOXLEY (1869-1955) and the local Hitchin architect GEOFFRY LUCAS (1872-1947). WILLIAM HARRISON COWLISHAW (1869-1957) contributed some more unusual buildings, including The Cloisters and the Theospohical Society's Vasanta Hall. Many other builders and architects are represented in the Cheap Cottages Exhibition and in the early developments. This talented generation of architects and town planners was given its head in Letchworth and went on to influence the style of urban development and housing not only in Britain but also in many other countries.

5. A RICH MIX OF PEOPLE

If you go to the churchyard of the old church of St Nicholas at Norton and walk past the church to the far side, where the fence overlooks the fields leading down towards Baldock, you find four gravestones with scrolled curved top edges. They face away from the church, so you need to go as far as the boundary fence to be able to read them. They are all well preserved, clearly adorned with a red, gold and black tricolor. Each bears the familiar legend 'mort pour la patrie'.

These are the graves of four Belgian soldiers killed in the First World War – Corporal Louis Ledoux and privates Alphonse Dumont, Denijs Thonissen and Sylvain Sortet. All died in the last year of the conflict, Ledoux being killed first,

Belgian refugees found a haven in Letchworth during the First World War. The Campers Road area (above) became known as Little Antwerp. For some Belgian soldiers, the Garden City was a haven only in death. This is one of a group of war graves in Norton churchyard.

in December 1917, and Sortet the last in June 1918. The four had been among the first wave of foreign immigrants into Letchworth in 1915. Belgian refugees from the German invasion of their country flooded into Britain from the end of 1914; the new town of Letchworth was building houses. Predominately, they came to live in the Campers Road area, which became dubbed 'Little Antwerp'. Their arrival swung the balance against the pacifist movement in Letchworth as the town became home to the Kryn and Lahy munitions works in Dunhams Lane, established by two Belgians to make shells for the allied armies and at the same time provide employment for their fellow countrymen

Although most of the 3,000 or so Belgians who came to the Garden City returned home after the Armistice, the factory – Letchworth's largest – remained and moved to peacetime activities as a steel foundry with a sister factory producing cranes under the name Jones Cranes, both in due course becoming part of the George Cohen 600 Group. During the Second World War the site again became a major arms factory.

The Kryn and Lahy factory is no more, but Letchworth's welcome to its Belgian guests is remembered in Howard Park where there is an oak tree, marked with a simple plaque, presented to the town by Albert I, King of the Belgians. There are more Belgian graves in St Mary's churchyard in old Letchworth.

The Belgian refugees were the first of a wave of immigrants. Many Poles came to the town as their country was torn apart by Germany and the Soviet Union in the Second World War; Italians, many originally employed in the Bedfordshire brick fields, moved in; Jewish refugees from Europe and evacuees from London (including the mother of Jack Cohen, founder of Tesco) found safety in the Garden City. And in the decades since the Second World War, the rich diversity of Letchworth's people has continued to develop, giving the town its lively racial and cultural mix.

Reflecting this, St. Hugh's Roman Catholic church had regular services in Polish, Sollershott East housed a synagogue, Gernon Walk is home to a Sikh temple, and High Avenue houses a Buddhist centre.

6. IDEAS AND INDUSTRY

John Buchan's *Mr Standfast,* published in 1919 and set during the First World War, has Richard Hannay, Buchan's hero, sent to pose as a pacifist in the thinly-disguised Garden City of Biggleswick, having been told by his contact: 'You have got to sink down into the life of the half-baked, the people whom this war

The Simple Life Hotel and Food Reform Restaurant in Leys Avenue would have been viewed with suspicion by Richard Hannay. This picture dates from about 1910.

hasn't touched or has touched in the wrong way, the people who split hairs all day and who are engrossed in what you and I would call selfish little fads...You won't live in an old manor...but among gimcrack little "arty" houses. You will hear everything you regard as sacred laughed at and condemned, and every kind of nauseous folly acclaimed.'

Hannay lodged in one of 200 houses built around a pleasant common. 'It was badly built and oddly furnished; the bed was too short, the windows did not fit, the doors did not stay shut.' The large garden was mainly given over to potatoes, since his hosts, the Jimsons, practised the simple life of self-sufficiency. Mr Jimson commuted to the city, but wore loose clothes, not the traditional starched city collars, while Mrs Jimson enthused over the merits of Garden City society: 'It is one great laboratory of thought. It is glorious to feel that you are living among eager and vital people who are at the head of all the newest movements, and that the intellectual history of England is being made in our studies and gardens. The war to us seems a remote and secondary affair. As someone has said, the great fights of the world are all fought in the mind.'

Hannay attends lectures and debates at The Moot, the local meeting place where the war is discussed in a detached manner, with the enemy case being debated even-handedly. Reporting back to his superior, however, Hannay concludes that the citizens are mostly harmless: 'A lot of ignorance, a large slice of vanity, and a pinch or two of wrong-headed honesty – these are the ingredients of the pie...You might plant a Biggleswick in every shire and it wouldn't help the Boche. These fellows talked academic anarchism, but the genuine article is somewhere about, and to find it you've got to look in the big industrial districts.' Thus Hannay is posted off to Clydeside in search of more serious subversives.

Buchan's satire has some element of truth. For many of the early pioneers came in search of a new lifestyle. The atmosphere of the earnest political and social debates that took place at the Howard Hall or at the Pixmore Institute no doubt rings true. And Buchan makes no reference to Letchworth's most unusual institution, The Cloisters, founded by Annie Lawrence to promote alternative lifestyles and radical thought, with real ambitions to change the world. The Garden City attracted many idealists and Letchworth nurtured many political, religious and social '-isms' – vegetarianism, teetotalism, internationalism, esperantism, Liberal Catholicism and theosophy.

Some pioneers were followers of the 'Simple Life' philosopher Edward Carpenter, a socialist whose ideals chimed with the Arts and Crafts promotion of honest labour with an advocacy of simple social forms. He lived quietly in Derbyshire, but one of his followers, George Adams, came to Letchworth and

39

set up as a sandal maker. In Edwardian times, sandals were a sign of rebellious-ness and belonged to Letchworth's 'rational dress' movement. Buchan's host Jimson may have been sufficiently daring to commute to the city in a loose fit-ting suit, soft collar and brightly coloured tie, but he was a pillar of conformity compared with the more extreme rational dressers who wore smocks, sandals and bare legs. Ethel Henderson's memoirs refer to the handsome young men at The Cloisters who wore this attire, earning the town some notoriety as visitors, including reporters from the national press, came for the cottage exhibitions. Some more adventurous spirits went further and paraded only in togas or loin-cloths. A famous cartoon of 1909 by Louis Weirter, entitled 'What outsiders think of us', depicts Londoners in fashionable Edwardian dress showing be-mused condescension to the native peasantry in their smocks, tilling the soil and living on nuts and fruit juice, served at the vegetarian hotel, the Simple Life Hotel in Leys Avenue.

Letchworth banned licensed premises within the town, the company hav-ing been visited in its early days by a deputation from the Temperance move-ment, and remained 'dry' without public houses except in the old villages of Norton and Willian and on the fringes of the Garden City until the 1960s. The Skittles Inn (now the Settlement) in Exhibition Road (now Nevells Road) was designed as an old-fashioned public house, but famously served only non-alcoholic drinks. Regular referendums maintained the dry status until 1961. Howard himself had proposed an experiment, with a public house at one side of the town only, allowing the effects of alcohol to be observed by contrasting that part with the dry part. In the event, the town provided a brisk trade for the delivery vans of nearby off-licences – and, according to Philip Purser's splendid evocation of early Letchworth in his story of Ebenezer Day in *The Last Great Tram Race* (published 1974), the home-made wines of the ladies of the Women's Institute.

Open-air living was another enthusiasm. Many houses, including Barry Parker's, had sleeping platforms – balconies for sleeping in the open air. The Cloisters' student sleeping quarters were open, and the first St Christopher School buildings (1919) allowed for open air classes.

Yet in reality, by the time *Mr Standfast* was published, utopian dreams were already dying, deflated by the experience of the First World War. There had been fierce debates at the Howard Hall between pacifists and patriots but Letchworth rapidly became involved in the war with soldiers billeted in the new houses before being shipped overseas and with the arrival of Belgian refugees bringing first hand accounts of the grim realities of war.

Even in the early days, indeed, the Garden City was a hive of economic activity, as its founders intended. An article in *The Times* of 1907 by J Penne said: 'I had imagined it (the Garden City) to be a new Eden, a City of Dreamers, the habitat of the simple life, where ideas and not realities were cultivated by men who wore velvet jackets, long hair and soft hats, and women who went hatless, dispensed with corsets and high heels, and wore everything that was "rational" regardless of fashion. I found the Garden City a city of work. Its men and women were just like other men and women, and its children differed from London children only in being chubbier, rosier and happier looking.'

The company's publicity, both in the early days and between the wars, emphasised Letchworth's advantages as a location for industry. Successive brochures listed the companies that had successfully transplanted to the new city – 24 in 1910, 52 by 1922 and well over 100 in the 1930s. A wide variety of industry was represented, including printing and bookbinding, vehicle manufacture, castings, transmission systems, instrumentation, furniture, embroidery, corsetry, baby carriages, and, between the wars, more modern trades such as parachutes, typewriters and tabulating machines, the information technology of the day. All the emphasis in the marketing of Letchworth was on the 'green field' advantages for business – low rates enabled factories to be built spaciously on a single floor to permit efficiency in production, there were siding connections to the railway, Letchworth was close to the principal market of London, and so on. In particular, Letchworth was a pleasant place to live for managers and workforce, who would all enjoy superior housing close to their places of work. Penne's report described visits to WH Smith bookbinders and to Healey Gresham Engineering, whose managers were happy to testify to these advantages. All this promotion of the new town was hard-headed and practical.

By the 1930s, Letchworth was an industrial success story. By late 1937, when the population was around 18,000, it was estimated that the factories employed 11,000 people. Around 4,000 people commuted in from the surrounding area. Kryn and Lahy was the largest single employer with around 1,500. In Pixmore Avenue, a factory owned by Ascot Motor Company closed in 1930 and was converted into a government training centre for the unemployed. By the second world war over 10,000 men and youths had passed through its training schemes, many from the depressed areas of the north of England and Wales. As a result of the depression, which left Letchworth relatively unscathed, the Ministry of Labour was involved in relocation schemes and would provide subsidised housing and removal costs for unemployed workers and their families from regions of high unemployment, assisted by directors of First Garden City

Parachute maker Irving Air Chute was an early Letchworth company. Its Californian founder was Leslie Irvin, but an extra 'g' was added as a result, it was said, of a typing error. Today, Irvin's name has been revived.

The Chater Lea building in Icknield Way. Founded in 1890, Chater Lea moved from London to Letchworth in 1928. Known for its lightweight motorcycle components, it also produced complete motorbikes and in London had also manufactured a few cars.

'Castle Corset', designed by Cecil Hignett and built between 1912 and 1922, housed corset manufacturer Spirella, also founded by an American. With its superb Arts and Crafts exterior, it has been magnificently restored.

Limited, who would help with presentations to audiences of unemployed men in those places.

World War Two gave industry a further boost. The Kryn and Lahy works returned to the manufacture of arms and ammunition, its offshoot Jones Cranes supplied the forces with the earliest mobile cranes, dustcart manufacturer Shelvoke and Drewry secretly manufactured midget submarines, and parachute manufacturer Irving Airchute stepped up its supplies for the Royal Air Force. The Urban District Council itself sponsored a Spitfire. Meanwhile the British Tabulating Machine Company was doing important work on decoding enemy signals.

Public policy, together with state directed planning, had moved on a stage further by the 1950s. Then, the local press reported a real possibility that Letchworth companies would be asked to transplant to areas of high unemployment as a price for being allowed to expand. None appears to have done so despite inducements. Yet the expansion continued and a survey by *The Citizen* in December 1964 reported that the town of 27,000 people employed 23,000, with between 10,000 and 12,000 commuting in. Kryn and Lahy hired two coaches daily from St Neots and one from Cambridge, and corset manufacturer Spirella, Irving Airchute, furniture producer D Meredew and automatic gearbox maker Borg Warner also provided buses for workers.

Pressure for development continued and in the 1960s Letchworth took its share of London overspill population as, in an updated version of Howard's intentions, London authorities sought to reduce their populations and to move people to more pleasant surroundings. *The Citizen* reported (September 24 1965) that Londoners would be moved out with their companies 'to the urban council's big new Jackmans estate being built on ultra-modern "pedestrian safety" lines in conjunction with the London authorities'. By 1968 the last designated industrial site was being developed in Blackhorse Road, to be occupied by businesses from London allocated by the Greater London Council.

It was the recession of the late 1970s and early 1980s that put an end to traditional industrial Letchworth as manufacturing industry in Britain started to shrink. The passing of the Kryn and Lahy steel foundry in August 1979, though a major loss, was by then relatively unlamented in *The Citizen*, which commented: 'In recent years it (the K&L works) has sometimes seemed ill at ease among North Herts industries which are increasingly science based, many of them working at the frontiers of electronic development.'

A brochure produced by the Garden City Corporation in 1980 sought to encourage industry to move to the town by extolling its virtues as a pleasant place of employment. It lists many of the famous names – ICL (International Computers, which had evolved from the British Tabulating Machine Company, known to generations simply as The Tab), pram manufacturer Marmet, Spirella, Jones Cranes and Shelvoke and Drewry are all there, but all were soon to succumb to the chilly draughts of economic reconstruction. Jones Cranes employed 1,000 people in three sites in 1980, and was down to 200 on one site in 1984, finally closing a year later. Marmet became part of the Restmor Group in 1973 and Britax-Restmor in 1987, its Letchworth site closing soon thereafter. Spirella limped on until 1989, a shadow of its former self. Relics of some of the big names remain – Marmet Close is on the site of the pram factory, while The Tab's striking art deco factory has given way to a housing development, Tabbs Court.

Today about half of Letchworth's working population work outside the town while about half the 15,000 people (according to the 2001 census) who work in Letchworth live elsewhere.

Electrification of the railway to London in 1972 brought a much faster and more frequent service – non-stop rush hour trains now take less than 30 minutes to Kings Cross – making commuting less unattractive. Between 06.30 and 08.30 each day about 1,200 people catch the train to London, with smaller numbers heading for Stevenage, Welwyn Garden City and Cambridge. Letchworth has become part of the London commuter belt, but it remains a significant home of modern business, midway between London and Cambridge's 'silicon fen'.

PART TWO

Only in Letchworth

Some Unique Garden City Institutions

1. Letchworth Garden City Heritage Foundation

Letchworth Garden City Heritage Foundation is the successor to the Garden City Corporation, which in turn had been the public sector successor to the private sector First Garden City Ltd. It operates alongside the elected local authorities: Hertfordshire County Council, North Hertfordshire District Council and Letchworth Town Council.

Created in 1995 after the government decided to remove the Corporation from the public sector, the Foundation is an 'industrial and provident society with charitable status', charged with generating cash from its assets, now mostly commercial property, to reinvest in charitable work within the town. Profits return to the community, giving supplementary funding for health, education, leisure and the arts, and providing grants to local clubs and societies, in line with Howard's vision. By the 1950s, enough had been raised to pay the dividends owing to the shareholders and small amounts became available for the original purpose of reinvesting in the town – a few thousands per year.

After the battle over First Garden City in 1962-3 and the takeover of the company, followed by the Parliamentary Act sponsored by Letchworth Urban District Council which brought the estate into public ownership, the newly created Corporation faced the payment of compensation to the old company. This was eventually agreed at £3,115,000 and took five years to pay. To eliminate its remaining debts to the council, the Corporation sold a large section of Standalone Farm land bordering the Grange Estate for housing, and it was from that point onwards that the surpluses started to reach the hundreds of thousands of pounds. Since then, the revenue stream has increased steadily. With assets of £114m, the Foundation's annual income exceeds £9m. In 2004-5, charitable spending totalled £1.8m.

The transition from the state Corporation to the private Foundation was not entirely smooth. Corporation critics had accused it of being aloof and unresponsive to concerns in the town. A battle over leasehold reform at the end of the 1960s created considerable controversy, which was resurrected with disputes over the charges levied for the purchase of home lease extensions and the purchase of freeholds. With the Corporation's demise, some questioned whether Letchworth needed a successor body to operate alongside the district

◄ One of Letchworth's most extraordinary buildings, The Cloisters in Barrington Road housed an extraordinary adult education centre. Built in 1906, the architect was WH Cowlishaw.

and county councils, with their powers over planning and development. The opposition went as far as evidence to the Parliamentary committee considering the bill to establish the Foundation.

There was particular difficulty reaching agreement on the new body's constitution. The Corporation's five board members were nominated by the government and the county and district councils. In an attempt to make the Foundation more representative and responsive, it has 30 governors – 14 appointed by the Board, six directly elected, eight nominated by various charitable and leisure groups within the town and one each by the county and district councils. The governors have a consultative role and elect six of their number to the eight-member board of management (the other two members are the governors representing the county and district councils).

Debate about the Foundation has continued. It has faced charges of heavy-handedness in the way it enforces its own planning rules, on such things, for example, as replacement windows in houses. Some of its property development has come under fire – the town council, established in 2005, had its origins in a row over the demolition of old stables to the north of the town to make way for housing. Plans for the redevelopment of much of the town centre have proved particularly controversial.

The distinction between commercial and charitable activities, normal in this sort of body, has the potential to create a tension, as it can do in other organisations with both business and philanthropic functions. Getting the balance right between a long-term vision for the town and short- and medium-term objectives, both commercial and charitable, may be a problem. Liaison with the district council has occasionally not been as smooth as it might be, though relations are generally good.

At the same time, such things as the day hospital, the town's cinema and the farm centre owe their existence or continued existence to the Foundation. It has made possible much beneficial re-development, been responsible for a major boost to leisure facilities, and given substantial help to local schools and many local clubs and other organisations. Total charitable spending since its inception has reached over £15 million. Its constitution charges it with:

> **Promoting the preservation of buildings and other environmental features of beauty or historic interest.**
> **Providing or assisting in the provision of facilities for recreation or other leisure activity in the interests of social welfare with the object of improving conditions of life.**

Promoting the advancement of education and learning.

Promoting the relief of poverty and sickness.

Supporting any charitable organisation having an office or branch in Letchworth.

Promoting any other charitable purposes for the benefit of the local community.

Architecture and Environment

The Foundation no longer owns the entire site on which Letchworth stands. It still owns much of the industrial and commercial land, including a large part of the town centre, but the Corporation started giving up its domestic leaseholds and selling freeholds in the wake of the 1967 Leasehold Reform Act. Now virtually all private houses are freehold. Under a scheme of management, however, most householders, outside the large former council estates of Grange and Jackmans, carrying out property alterations need Foundation approval to ensure the architectural character of the town is preserved. The vast majority of proposals are approved, and grants are available to help with improvements or renovation that meet Garden City guidelines.

Other projects have included assistance with the district council's remodelling of the Broadway gardens in the town centre, the Greenway pathway around the town, the Settlement adult education centre (external redecoration) and help both for the ancient St Mary's Church in old Letchworth and with the more modern St George's Church in Norton Way North.

Recreation and Leisure

The Corporation and subsequently the Foundation have long been involved in the provision of sporting amenities. The Leisure Centre, opened by The Queen in 1982, is now run by the District Council but was a Corporation initiative. More recently, the Heritage Foundation has transformed the former ICL playing fields in Whitethorn Lane, which now, under the umbrella of Letchworth Corner Sports Club, provide a home for the cricket club, hockey club, bowls, weightlifting, football and the running club. Substantial Heritage Foundation support also ensured superb facilities for the Tennis Club when it moved to Muddy Lane.

Scouting and Guiding have frequently benefited from Foundation money. The biggest single scheme was the provision in 2003 of a £320,000 HQ and

The First Garden City Heritage Museum, converted from Parker and Unwin's offices and supported by the Heritage Foundation – as have been the Broadway Gardens and St Mary's below.

Broadway Gardens as transformed in 2005.

St Mary's, Letchworth, 12th century.

activity centre at Wymondley Wood to replace a facility at Norton Bury, which has been converted into housing.

The Foundation is also a major provider of funds to Letchworth Arts Centre (formerly the Place) in the town centre and, working with North Herts District Council through the Letchworth Garden City Arts Partnership, has recently helped to oversee an extensive refurbishment programme that has greatly improved facilities and enabled an exciting range of events.

Four sizeable enterprises are run by the Foundation directly: Plinston Hall, a venue for concerts, exhibitions and entertainment; the First Garden City Heritage Museum, converted from Parker and Unwin's offices in Norton Way South, which records the history of the Garden City (and may move to the now surplus Town Hall in the centre of the town, along with the Tourist Information Centre, to provide substantially expanded facilities); Standalone Farm; and the three-screen Broadway Cinema.

Education and Learning

Grants are available to all Letchworth schools for such items as IT facilities, and recent awards have been for improved internet access, interactive whiteboards and other equipment. Education 2000 was an innovative scheme for the provision of computer equipment for schools, using a shared IT network.

It has been contributing £10,000 a year to the Letchworth Civic Trust toward top-up grants to university students.

Relief of Poverty and Sickness

The cornerstone here is the unique Ernest Gardiner Day Hospital. Opened in 1984, it is a private sector unit, with professional medical staff whose salaries are funded by the Foundation. Patients, who must be Letchworth or Baldock residents (Baldock Rotarians having been involved in the hospital's setting-up) and referred by their GP, pay nothing.

The hospital treats patients who are recovering from strokes or other illnesses and who need recuperation before being restored to independence. Priority tends to be given to patients living on their own.

The Foundation also manages a 'Shopmobility' scheme providing around 200 registered users with motorised wheelchairs to get round the town centre. These are collected at the Tourist Information Centre in Station Road.

Substantial support has been given to organisations such as the Letchworth

Three further recipients of support from the Heritage Foundation and its predecessor, the Letchworth Garden City Corporation. The art deco Broadway Cinema, splendidly restored and modernised, owes its continued existence to the Foundation, which runs it directly.

The North Herts Leisure Centre in Baldock Road, run by North Hertfordshire District Council, was a Garden City Corporation initiative.

Standalone Farm Centre on the northern edge of the Garden City off Wilbury Road is another Heritage Foundation enterprise.

Centre for Healthy Living, the Multiple Sclerosis Centre and the Young Home-lessness Group.

Supporting Charities

This has tended to be the smallest part of the Foundation's activity. Beneficiaries have included such bodies as the St John Ambulance Brigade, Headway, Relate, the Citizens Advice Bureau and the Lions Club.

Small Grants

A continuous flow of smaller grants goes out to many groups and individuals – children's and youth activities, churches, elderly associations, music groups, and so on.

The Foundation has five trading subsidiaries. LGC Farms, based at Manor Farm, Willian, runs the agricultural estate, whose predominantly arable prod-ucts are sold in the open market. It is responsible for Standalone Farm.

LGC Services provides catering at Plinston Hall, the Spirella Ballroom and café, and retails souvenirs through the Tourist Information Centre. It has a con-trolling interest in Broadway Cinema, another subsidiary.

Garden City Technologies provides technical and computing services in the Spirella building and other commercial properties owned by the Foundation. Finally there is Letchworth Cottages and Buildings, the housing association founded by the original company in 1906, although its activities are diminish-ing as the Foundation has decided to divest itself of most of its social housing.

The Foundation has also, in conjunction with North Herts Council, ap-pointed a town centre manager, who works with the owners of the central shop-ping development, the district council and shopkeepers to improve facilities and attract trade.

As mentioned earlier, it is currently embarking on a major regeneration plan for the town centre.

2. St Christopher School

One of Letchworth's most distinctive institutions is St Christopher School, founded in 1915 as a 'progressive' school by the Letchworth resident Ada Hope Rea, a theosophist who had been influenced by that movement while in India.

Especially influential were the ideas of George Arundale who preached education as service to society. Feeling that the new garden city would provide a fertile ground for a school based on theosophist principles, she secured financial support from wealthy benefactors and the school opened in January 1915 in a house in Broadwater Avenue. It moved to larger quarters in Barrington Road that August, taking over the building used by the original Letchworth School, which was duly renamed Arundale.

Under a charismatic headmaster named Armstrong Smith, the Garden City Theosophical School, as it was then known, set trends in progressive education. Formal discipline did not exist; the pupils were expected to discipline themselves and peer pressure was the principal means of control. Teachers were to guide pupils towards information so that children discovered for themselves rather than having information thrust upon them. Even truancy was tolerated – in the words of the school historian Reginald Snell: 'Once playing truant was permitted, it lost its attraction.'

The school was not, however, doctrinaire. The only guiding theosophist principle was that everyone else's beliefs should be respected and within that rule there was complete freedom of expression. One of Armstrong Smith's main preoccupations was that there should be no 'gossip', which he saw as a principal curse of childhood.

An element of self-government by the pupils was established by the formation of the Moot, a school council that had considerable powers of discipline and over the organisation of activities. Practical trades were taught through craft guilds, which were established in the early 1920s in tailoring, carpentry, maintenance and agriculture, led by professional craftsmen. Although after a few years these were closed by the trustees as unviable, one, originally the school's own printing press, survived until the 1970s as the independent St Christopher Press.

On September 25 1919 the foundation stone of a new building in Broadway was laid by the Theosophist leader Annie Besant. The building, now named the St Christopher School, opened a year later under a merger with the Letchworth Modern School for Girls, with Arundale remaining as the boarding house. The Broadway buildings featured open-air galleries for outdoor teaching and study. In 1925 a large theatre was added, opened by the actress Ellen Terry.

Armstrong Smith's reign was relatively short; ill health forced his retirement in 1919. He was succeeded eventually by Isobel King, headmistress of the girls' school. Miss King, with another benefactor Beatrice Ensor, moved on to found a second similar school in Surrey and between 1925 and 1954 the school was

Now part of St Christopher School, Arunside, dating from 1904-05, was originally two houses, designed by Parker and Unwin as their own homes, and subsequently became a school boarding house.

under the headmastership of Henry Lyn Harris, who moved it back to Barrington Road and steered it to independence in 1930 after a dispute with the trustees. From then on, the school was no longer primarily theosophical. Lyn Harris being a Quaker, the educational emphasis moved imperceptibly towards the Quaker principle of 'answering to that of God in every child'. The school maintained its progressive principles while attaining recognition as an 'efficient secondary school' from the Ministry of Education, the 1930s equivalent of an Ofsted stamp of approval.

In recent years, the school has faced the difficult task of maintaining a distinctive ethos while meeting the need for students to succeed in higher education and in employment in an ever more competitive world. But, with its continuing principles of non-competitive schooling, with 'each pupil being taught to value their own and each other's efforts and growing achievements', co-educational boarding, and vegetarianism, it remains an example of an early Letchworth socio-educational experiment that has outlived others such as its neighbour, The Cloisters (see below and *Walk 3*) and the Skittles Inn (now the Settlement; see *Walk 1*).

St Christopher has, of course, only ever catered for a minority of Letchworth children and most pupils come from elsewhere. The majority of Letchworth children have always been catered for by the state secondary sector, first by The Norton School, then the Grammar School built on the town square and opened in 1931, then in the postwar expansion by The Highfield School in the west and The Willian School on the Jackmans Estate in the south east of the town. Meanwhile, St Christopher's Broadway site was taken over in 1934 by a Catholic teaching order, the Sisters of Charity, and expanded with its present buildings to form St Francis' College, an independent boarding and day school for girls. The Grammar School closed in 1963 when the new Fearnhill comprehensive school opened in Icknield Way.

Population changes resulted in the closures first of Willian (1988) and then of Norton (2003).

3. THE CLOISTERS

The Cloisters, in Barrington Road, is one of Letchworth's most extraordinary buildings. The institution it once housed was equally extraordinary, an idealistic adult education centre whose founder Annie Lawrence wanted visitors to come to the new City to experience what today would be called alternative lifestyles. Built in 1906 and designed by W H Cowlishaw, the building, open to the air, provided Spartan sleeping accommodation for 20 people in hammocks. There were an organ, roof terraces, and an oval swimming pool. Within the building were fountains for semi-ceremonial washing. The marble floors both upstairs and at ground level were drained in such a way that they could be cleaned by hosing down.

Annie Lawrence came from a wealthy London family, her grandfather having arrived there from Cornwall and, in a rags-to-riches career, making a fortune as a master carpenter. Two of her uncles became Lord Mayors of London and her father was a proprietor of the City Ironworks. The family, who were Unitarians, immersed themselves in church and charity work. From her experiences working with London children, Annie Lawrence resolved to help them to a more inspiring and healthier life and the idea of The Cloisters

Spartan sleeping accommodation in hammocks, open-air classrooms and roof terraces characterised the remarkable Cloisters building.

was born. She decided that the best way to achieve her aims was to teach the teachers the principles of healthy living, and The Cloisters became aimed at adults, not children.

Cowlishaw, the architect, was in no doubt as to the revolutionary purpose of the project. He wrote in the Architectural Review: 'This building...has an essential bearing on the evolution of the human race. A School of Psychology is to be founded there, which will have for its principal object the study of "how thought affects action and what causes and produces thought"...It is intended that the students shall form the nucleus of an altruistic crusade against the low spiritual and corresponding economic state of the country.'

Between 1907 and 1912 courses were run by J. Bruce Wallace, founder of an organisation known as the Alpha Union, which was dedicated to radical thought. They included psychology and progressive religion, as well as more conventional studies of English and History. The course work was, however, a small part of the day, which was punctuated by callisthenics and dancing, with time for private meditation, while residents were encouraged to take part in craft activities and gardening. Midday meals were provided but, for the rest, students were left to their own devices. One Californian visitor is said to have lived on a diet of oranges. Miss Lawrence developed, and expected her guests to enact, the concept of the dual day, one part being devoted to work and the other to leisure and meditation.

The concept of The Cloisters was at one with the Arts and Crafts movement, promoting a simple life and the taking of pleasure in everyday things.

Though Bruce Wallace stopped his courses in 1912, courses in adult education continued after the First World War, concentrating on crafts such as weaving and basketwork. By now, there was less desire to change the world. The Cloisters became a more mainstream cultural centre offering open-air concerts, plays and shows, which attracted enthusiastic audiences from all classes. Local brass bands and orchestras played almost every week during the summer months and the building was used by the uniformed organisations. Swimming lessons were available in the oval pool, the only one in town at that time, and this facility was regularly used by the neighbouring St Christopher School.

Eventually the ageing Miss Lawrence, who had no heirs, became concerned about the future of the building. In 1933 she offered it free to Hertfordshire County Council, which, while appreciating the offer, was unable to fit it into its educational programme. Commandeered by the army in the Second World War, it fell into a dilapidated state but was sold to the Freemasons in 1948. The Freemasons have enclosed the sleeping area and converted it into a temple. The swimming pool was filled in in 1962 and is now the site of the warden's flat.

Annie Lawrence died in 1953 at the age of 90 and is buried in Willian churchyard.

4. David's Bookshops

David's, publisher of this guide, is one of Letchworth's oldest established retailers and one of the largest booksellers between London and Cambridge.

The original shop opened in 1963 in small premises in Station Place. Today, there are three shops: the main bookshop at 14 Eastcheap, the music shop next door at 12 Eastcheap, and the children's books, cards and gift shop opposite at 7 Eastcheap. Having an independent bookseller with so broad a range is highly unusual for a town of this size.

Browsing for bargains: pavement stalls are a popular feature of David's main bookshop.

David's organises a range of special events, normally in the bookshop, with author signings, book readings, discussions and poetry evenings, and also regularly holds David's debates on topical issues at larger venues. Book fairs are regularly held at local schools and elsewhere.

David's innovative approach and range of events, both in its shops and in the wider community, received national recognition when it beat the major bookselling chains to win the Marketing Campaign of the Year award in the 2006 competitions organised by *The Bookseller*. David's was the only independent bookshop to be shortlisted.

David's was behind the establishment of Letchworth Arts and Leisure Group, an umbrella organisation for a host of leisure and cultural activities, which is centred on the main Bookshop.

Music

David's Music is Letchworth's hugely popular independent record store. Catering for all tastes from the latest chart albums to jazz and classical, it has a large secondhand section, including a wide selection of vinyl, and friendly, knowledgeable staff.

Live bands play regularly at the shop, and it also helps to sponsor local music festivals.

It stocks a broad range of music books and sheet music, videos and DVDs, and record accessories. You can browse – and buy – online at www.davids-music.co.uk.

Books

Open seven days a week, the Bookshop carries a vast stock spread across two floors. You will find a comprehensive range of fiction, non-fiction, textbooks, maps and best-sellers. Travellers, walkers, computer users and local historians are especially well catered for. We can supply any book in print and there are always many titles on special offer.

There is a large secondhand and antiquarian department, mostly on the second floor. The book collector or second-hand browser can also check out a growing selection of our 15,000 secondhand and antiquarian books available for purchase through the internet.

If you have good quality books to sell bring them in for a quick appraisal and a fair offer. The staff really know about books and you can rely on their advice. You can also browse and buy online at www.davids-bookshops.co.uk.

Children's Books, Cards and Gifts

If you are seeking an elusive quality gift, a children's book, or just browsing for a greetings card, David's Gift Shop has one of the best selections of quality giftware in the area.

The Gift Shop is especially well known for its extensive range of cards, many hand-made. The children's book section appeals to all ages and reading levels.

PART THREE

A Letchworth Directory

A LETCHWORTH DIRECTORY

The Garden City pioneer Sir Frederic Osborn was once reported as saying it was a myth that there was no-one in Letchworth town centre in the evening; it was just that at 10 o'clock they both went home.

He was talking in the days when Letchworth was a 'dry' town. Since then, a handful of pubs and wine bars has opened, along with a selection of restaurants ranging from Thai, Italian, Mexican, Indian and Chinese to fish and chips, coffee bars, etc. But the town centre remains quiet compared with the neighbouring towns of Hitchin and Stevenage, and young people in particular tend to look there for evening entertainment rather than Letchworth.

Nonetheless, the town centre has a reasonable range of specialist shops, in addition to a supermarket and branches of national chains. There is also a three-screen cinema. But, apart from the supermarket, it lacks large stores. The principal shopping streets – Leys Avenue, Eastcheap, Station Road, Broadway, The Wynd, The Arcade linking Leys Avenue and Station Road, and the Arena – range round the Garden Square shopping centre, opened in the 1970s at the town's heart. Avoiding the concrete brutalism of so many post-war shopping developments it includes a covered market, while a farmers' market is held at its entrance in Leys Square on the third Saturday of every month, with regular French and Italian markets there too.

There are also two adjacent small out of town shopping centres, one also with a large supermarket, in the industrial area.

Plans are afoot for a major redevelopment of a sizeable part of the town centre which, if all goes ahead, will see the Arena and parts of Broadway and Eastcheap transformed, with underground car-parking, the potential for at least one large department store or similar, and a food court area with restaurants and cafes, and facilities for open air eating and drinking.

The plans also envisage big changes for The Wynd, which currently houses a number of interesting, specialist shops as well as an excellent Thai restaurant but in a generally rundown environment despite a more modern development at one end. The aim is for that to continue to house smaller, specialist shops, possibly with a food and cookery theme, as well as a children's play centre and underground parking.

◄ Exotic shopping: an international market adds variety to Eastcheap.
Sadly, these are unusual events

Inevitably, the scheme, a Garden City Heritage Foundation project, has aroused controversy. There have been fears that independent shops could be at risk, with individuality vanishing and chain stores of the type that dominate so many high streets taking over.

The Foundation has acknowledged the concerns and has said it will endeavour, subject to commercial realities, to assuage them. The outcome remains to be seen. Details of the proposals and progress on them can be found at www. thenextsteps.co.uk.

Country Pubs

Although the town centre was 'dry' until the 1960s, the fringes of the town have long been provided with public houses. At Willian are The Fox, which has a separate restaurant, and The Three Horseshoes. Both long pre-date the Garden City, as does The Three Horseshoes at Norton. Letchworth Hall Hotel, originally a 15th century manor house, in Letchworth Lane has a pleasant bar open to non-residents. Just outside the original Garden City boundaries are the Wilbury, Wilbury Hills Road, and the Two Chimneys, Stotfold Road.

Hotels

BROADWAY, Broadway (01462 480111; www.broadwayhotel.co.uk)
GARDEN LODGE, Sollershott East (01462 685100)
LETCHWORTH HALL, Letchworth Lane, old Letchworth
    (01462 683747); www.aquariushotels.co.uk
SLEEP INN, AI (M), Baldock Services/Radwell junction
    (01462 832900); www.hotels-baldock.com
TRAVELODGE, A1, Hinxworth (0870 1911505); www.travelodge.co.uk

Camping and Caravanning

RADWELL MILL LAKE (01462 730253).

Clubs & Societies

Events listings can be found in the Heritage Foundation's quarterly *Spotlight* newsletter, which typically lists over 30 clubs and societies catering for all ages, and a similar number of events or excursions per month. Letchworth Arts and

Leisure Group, centred on David's Bookshop in Eastcheap, is an umbrella organisation for a host of activities, with meetings and events listed in its monthly newsletter. Copies go to members and can also be obtained at David's Bookshop. David's Bookshop and the adjacent David's Music shop also have noticeboards listing events.

PLINSTON HALL on Broadway Gardens, is a prime music venue with discos and live performances by tribute bands and more sedate events such as ballroom dancing, including tea dances. It also hosts a number of clubs and societies and has its own café, open to the general public, and bar.
(01462 672003); www.plinstonlive.com

LETCHWORTH ARTS CENTRE (formerly the Place) in the Arcade has recently been refurbished by the Letchworth Garden City Arts Partnership, which brings together the Garden City Heritage Foundation and North Herts District Council, and plans an exciting programme of exhibitions, theatrical and musical performances and educational events.
(01462 670788); www.placearts.org

THE SETTLEMENT adult education centre in Nevells Road has its own theatre group, the Settlement Players, hosts a number of weekly and monthly organisations such as the Camera Club and the local RSPB Group, and offers courses on a wide range of subjects.(01462 682828);
www.pages.britishlibrary.net/Letchworthsettlement/ index.html

BROADWAY CINEMA at the corner of Gernon Road and Eastcheap, is a refurbished art deco cinema and has three screens. As well as general release films, it holds regular retro screenings. Once a month the award-winning Letchworth Film Club takes over one of its screens.
(01462 681223); www.broadway-cinema.com

MUSEUM AND ART GALLERY adjacent to the LIBRARY (01438 737333) facing Broadway Gardens has a natural history display on the ground floor and local archaeological remains on the first floor, with a changing programme of special exhibitions in its galleries.
(01462 685647); www.north-herts.gov.uk/leisure

FIRST GARDEN CITY HERITAGE MUSEUM Norton Way South, housed in what were Parker and Unwin's drawing offices and Barry Parker's home, covers the history of Letchworth Garden City and often has special exhibitions. A move to more central premises, possibly shared with the Museum and Art Gallery, is under discussion (01462 482710);
www.letchworthgc.com/ placestovisit/history/gardencityheritagemuseum.html

STANDALONE FARM CENTRE Wilbury Road, is a small working show farm on an open site on the edge of the town. Oriented toward young families, it is home to a good selection of farm animals, along with a pets' corner for young children. Barns house historic machinery, you can watch the cows being milked, and there are regular special exhibitions as well as pleasant walks into the surrounding countryside. It is open from April to October.
(01462 686775)
www.letchworthgc.com/placestovisit/ history/standalonefarm.html

Sports Facilities

THE NORTH HERTS LEISURE CENTRE Baldock Road, has a swimming pool with a flume and a nursery pool and also provides a gym and sauna, squash courts and a games hall used for badminton, judo, roller-skating and many other activities.
(01462 679311); www.north-herts.gov.uk/leisure

Adjacent to the Leisure Centre are the RUGBY CLUB
(01462 682554); www.letchworthrugby.com
and the GARDEN CITY EAGLES a youth football club catering for boys and girls across a wide age range, with several teams.
(01462 672075); letchwortheagles.org.uk

The FOOTBALL GROUND in Baldock Road is the headquarters of the COUNTY FOOTBALL ASSOCIATION
(01462 677622); www.hertfordshirefa.com
Opposite is the BALDOCK ROAD RECREATION GROUND.

THE CRICKET CLUB is in Whitethorn Lane. It is one of the constituent clubs of the Letchworth Corner Sports Club. The club has a second ground at Fairfield

Park on the outskirts of Letchworth.
(01462 684530); www.letchworth.play-cricket.com

THE HOCKEY CLUB is also at Letchworth Corner Sports Club in Whitethorn
Lane. (01462 684530); www.letchworth-hockey.org

HITCHIN WEIGHTLIFTING CLUB is also based at Letchworth Corner Sports
Club in Whitethorn Lane.(01462 675952)

THE TENNIS CLUB has purpose built premises in Muddy Lane, opened in 2005
by the Duchess of Gloucester, with indoor and outdoor courts, a dedicated children's zone, a crèche and a wide range of other facilities, including a gymna-
sium and fitness centre.
(01462 675444); www.letchworthtennisclub.co.uk)

LETCHWORTH CORNER SQUASH CLUB shares facilities with the tennis club and
has two courts.
(01462 675444); www.lcsc.mysite.wanadoo-members.co.uk

LETCHWORTH CROQUET CLUB also shares facilities with the tennis club and has
two laser-levelled lawns.
(01462 673375); www.letchworthcroquetclub.co.uk

LETCHWORTH GOLF CLUB has an 18-hole course in Letchworth Lane, old Letchworth. The course, extended in 2003, is one of the county's leading golf courses
and is extremely picturesque.
(01462 683203); www.letchworthgolfclub.com
There is a popular PUBLIC COURSE outside the town on the old Great North
Road at Chesfield Downs. (01462 482929); www.chesfielddownsgolf.com
THE FAMILY GOLF CENTRE in Willian Way has a par three course.
(01462 483683)

NORTH HERTS ROAD RUNNERS is Letchworth's well-supported running club,
which caters for all ages and abilities. NHRR, based at Letchworth Corner
Sports Club in Whitethorn Lane, has had a number of competitive successes in
national competitions. (01462 684530; www.nhrr.org.uk),
    Its biggest event of the year is the Standalone 10K one of the biggest annual

running events in Hertfordshire.(www.standalone1ok.org.uk)

There are several bowling greens (www.mixedbowls.co.uk). LETCHWORTH GARDEN CITY BOWLS CLUB (01462 632171) is at Norton Common off Icknield Way. Norton Common also houses NORTH HERTS BOWLS CLUB (01462 636085) and WILLIAN BOWLS CLUB (01462 683189). HOWARD GARDEN BOWLS CLUB (01462 685864) is in Norton Way South. NORTON BOWLS CLUB (01462 635243) has its green at the Three Horseshoes, Norton Road. WHITETHORN BOWLS CLUB (01462 631637) is at Letchworth Corner Sports Club in Whitethorn Lane. THE SHORT MAT BOWLS CLUB (01462 685746) meets at the North Herts Leisure Centre, Baldock Road.

The heated open air SWIMMING POOL is on Norton Common, open summer only. (01462 684673)

Norton Common also has PUBLIC TENNIS COURTS, a PUTTING GREEN, and a CHILDREN'S PLAY AREA. There is another CHILDREN'S PLAYGROUND in Howard Park, along with a CHILDREN'S PADDLING POOL (summer only), and a PUTTING GREEN at Howard Garden. There are PLAYING FIELDS at Gaunts Way on the Grange Estate and Radburn Way on the Jackmans Estate, and a RECREATION GROUND at Temple Gardens. There is another CHILDREN'S PLAY AREA at Hillbrow and another RECREATION GROUND in Baldock Road.

Gyms

NORTH HERTS LEISURE CENTRE (01462 679311), Baldock Road
FEARNHILL SPORTS CENTRE (01462 676017), Icknield Way West
SPIRELLA FITNESS CENTRE (01462 476123); www.spirella.com/gym.htm), Bridge Road
CANNONS (01462 681075), Letchworth Lane (adjacent to Letchworth Hall Hotel)
LETCHWORTH TENNIS CLUB, Muddy Lane
(01462 675444); www. letchworthtennisclub. co.uk

Function Rooms and Halls for Hire

BROADWAY HOTEL, Broadway (01462 480111); www.broadwayhotel.co.uk

LETCHWORTH HALL HOTEL, Letchworth Lane (01462 6837470); www.aquariushotels.co.uk

PLINSTON HALL, Broadway (01462 672003); www.plinston.com

SPIRELLA BALLROOM, Bridge Road (01462 650141); www.spirella.com

BROTHERHOOD HALL, Gernon Road (not licensed). North Herts Council: (01462 434658)CENTRAL METHODIST CHURCH HALL, Norton Way South (01462 481658)

GRANGE COMMUNITY CENTRE, Middlefields (01462 620505) (mornings only)

HOWGILLS (Society of Friends), South View (01462 484518)

JACKMANS COMMUNITY CENTRE, Ivel Court (01462 6425250

LETCHWORTH FREE CHURCH HALL, Gernon Road (01462 682568)

LETCHWORTH SETTLEMENT, Nevells Road (01462 682828); www.pages.britishlibrary.net/letchworthsettlement/index.html

NORTH HERTS LEISURE CENTRE, Baldock Road (01462 679723)

NORTON METHODIST COMMUNITY CENTRE, North Avenue (01462 631169)

NORTON PARISH CENTRE, Norton Way North (01462 678133)

ST PAUL'S CHURCH HALL, Pixmore Way (01462 637373); www.stpaulsletchworth.co.uk

WILBURY CHURCH HALL, Bedford Road (01462 679646); www.stthomasletchworth.org.uk

WILBURY HALL, Bedford Road (01462 676408) (Monday evenings only)

WILLIAN VILLAGE HALL, Willian (01462 685712)

Education

NURSERIES AND NURSERY SCHOOLS

GLEBE KIDS 30 Glebe Rd (01462 686683)

GRANGE TINY HANDS PRE-SCHOOL, Middlefields (01462 627333)

HILLSHOTT (*see* Primary Schools)

ICKNIELD (*see* Primary Schools)

Leapfrog Day Nursery, Icknield Way (01462 683761; www.leapfrogday nurseries.co.uk)

LORDSHIP FARM (*see* Primary Schools)

NEVELLS ROAD NURSERY SCHOOL, Nevells Rd (01462 684813)

NORTHFIELDS (*see* Primary Schools)

SKOOL'S OUT (www.skoolsout.com): Lordship Centre, Howard Drive (01462 677088), Howard Hall, Norton Way South (07876 728018)

Tom's Tots (for 1-3 years olds), Wilbury Hall, Bedford Road (01462 637718)
Westbury (*see* Primary Schools)
Wonderland Day Nursery, Works Rd (01462 480884).

Primary Schools

Grange JM, Sparhawke (01462 621444; www.grange.herts.sch.uk)
Hillshott Infants School and Nursery School, Ridge Avenue
    (01462 621212; www.hillshott.herts.sch.uk)
Icknield Infant and Nursery School, Archers Way
    (01462 620406; www.icknieldinfants.sch.uk)
Lannock JMI School, Whiteway (01462 620400;
    www.lannock.herts.sch.uk)
Lordship Farm JMI School (incorporates Lordship Farm Nursery School),
    Four Acres (01462 620550; www.lordshipfarm.org.uk)
Northfields Infant and Nursery School, Burley
    (01462 623388; www.northfield.herts.sch.uk)
Norton St Nicholas Church of England (Voluntary aided), Norton
    Road, Norton (01462 623322; www.stnicholas23.herts.sch.uk)
Pixmore JMI School, Rushby Mead
    (01462 620555; www.pixmore.herts.sch.uk)
Radburn JMI School, Radburn Way
    (01462 621800; www.radburn.herts.sch.uk)
St Thomas More Roman Catholic (Voluntary Aided), Highfield
    (01462 620670; strc.jmi.herts.sch.uk)
Stonehill JMI School, Western Close
    (01462 620262; www.cabletel-schools.org.uk/stonehilljmischool)
Westbury JMI & Nursery School, West View
    (01462 620300; www.westbury.herts.sch.uk)
Wilbury JMI School, Bedford Road
    (01462 620410; www.wilbury.herts.sch.uk)
Woolgrove School (for children with moderate learning difficulties), Pryor
    Way (01462 622422; atschool.eduweb.co.uk/woolgrov/index.html)

Comprehensive Schools

Fearnhill School, Icknield Way (01462 621200;
    www.fearnhill.herts.sch.org)

THE HIGHFIELD SCHOOL (01462 620500;
www.atschools.eduweb.co.uk/highfield).

INDEPENDENT SCHOOLS

ST CHRISTOPHER SCHOOL (boys and girls; Montessori department; Junior
school; Secondary school), Barrington Road
(01462 650850; www.stchris.co.uk)

ST FRANCIS' COLLEGE (girls aged 3-18; multi-denominational Christian),
Broadway (01462 670511; www.st-francis.herts.sch.uk).

Further Education

NORTH HERTS COLLEGE (01462 424239; www.nhc.ac.uk) runs business-related
courses at its Goldsmith Centre (01462 650250) in Broadway, and has other,
bigger sites at Hitchin and Stevenage.

THE SETTLEMENT, Nevells Road (01462 682828; www.pages.britishlibrary.net/
letchworthsettlement/index.html) offers a wide range of leisure activities and
adult education courses, some with syllabuses set by Cambridge University.

Places of Worship

CHURCH OF ENGLAND

LETCHWORTH PARISH CHURCH is ST MICHAEL'S, built in the late 1960s, in
Broadway. The parish also includes the ancient church of ST MARY in
Letchworth Lane, old Letchworth.
(01462 684822)

ST PAUL'S PARISH CHURCH (01462 637373; www.stpaulsletchworth.co.uk) on
the corner of Baldock Road and Pixmore Way, built in the early days of the
Garden City but never completed, serves the south east of the town; the
parish also includes the ancient church of ALL SAINTS at Willian.

ST GEORGE'S CHURCH in Norton Way North (01462 678133; www.letchworth-
gardencity.net/norton/index.html) was built in the 1960s and is the parish
church for the Norton parish. The parish covers the north of the town and
includes the original parish church of ST NICHOLAS in Norton village.

ST THOMAS OF CANTERBURY (01462 623119; www.stthomasletchworth.org.uk) in Bedford Road is the parish church for the Wilbury area.

ROMAN CATHOLIC

The imposing Roman Catholic Church of ST HUGH OF LINCOLN (01462 683504) faces St Michael's across the Broadway Gardens. Close by it is the attractive original Catholic church, now the church hall.

NONCONFORMIST

One of Letchworth's most interesting religious buildings is Howgills, the FRIENDS MEETING HOUSE (01462 484518) at 42 South View, designed by Bennett and Bidwell.

NORTH AVENUE METHODIST CHURCH (01462 646562) stems from the Norton Mission, founded by the famous Victorian preacher Gipsy Smith. The dedication to his parents can be seen in the church, along with wooden carvings in the form of gipsy caravans.

THE FREE CHURCH (United Reform Church) (01462 433693) in Gernon Road was designed by Barry Parker.

In Norton Way South is the simple, little LIBERAL CATHOLIC CHURCH OF ST ALBAN (01462 623658), which also houses an Old Anglican congregation.

Other Letchworth churches include the CENTRAL METHODIST in Norton Way South (01462 646562; www.letchworth-central-methodist.info); the BAPTIST in West View (01462 482780), GRANGE BAPTIST CHURCH in Danescroft (01462 679498); www.grangebaptist.org), and the SALVATION ARMY HALL (01462 677263) in Norton Way North. The NEW LIFE CHURCH (01462 680188; www.nlcletchworth.co.uk) holds prayer meetings at Howard Hall, and the LETCHWORTH GARDEN CITY CHURCH (ELIM) is in Icknield Way East (01462 480126; www.lgcitychurch.net). On the Jackmans Estate, KINGS BAPTIST CHURCH (01462 730521) is in Whiteway.

OTHERS

BUDDHIST TEMPLE, 32 High Avenue
(01462 641326; www.letchworthtemple.com)
DHAMMA NIKETHANAYA BUDDHIST CENTRE, 69 Pix Road
    (01462 641688; www.letchworthbuddhism.com)
NANAKSAR SAR THATH ISHAR DARBAR (Sikh temple), 7 Gernon Walk
    (01462 684153)

SIRI GURU SINGH SABAR GURDWARA (Sikh temple), Icknield Way East
(01462 685029)

LETCHWORTH SPIRITUALIST CHURCH meets at Vasanta Hall, an unusual little
building in Gernon Walk designed by W H Cowlishaw, who also built The
Cloisters.

VASANTA HALL is also the home of LETCHWORTH THEOSOPHICAL SOCIETY
the local lodge of a movement dedicated to uniting religions by taking the
best wisdom of each.
(01438 722173)

Medical Facilities

DOCTORS' SURGERIES

BIRCHWOOD SURGERY, 232-240 Nevells Road (0844 477 3328)
GARDEN CITY SURGERY, 59 Station Road
    (01462 624000; www.gardencitysurgery.org.uk)
NEVELLS ROAD SURGERY, Nevells Road (0844 477 1796)
SOLLERSHOTT SURGERY, 44 Sollershott East (01462 683637)

DENTAL SURGERIES

COMMUNITY DENTAL CLINIC, Nevells Road (01462 682016)
185 Nevells Road (01462 481881)
12a Eastcheap (01462 679888)
49 Station Road (01462 684040)
125 Norton Way South (01462 683241)

HEALTH CENTRE

NEVELLS ROAD HEALTH CENTRE (01462 684731)
LETCHWORTH MENTAL HEALTH TEAM, St Michael's House, Norton Way
    South (01462 482982)

HOMOEOPATHIC

LETCHWORTH CENTRE FOR HEALTHY LIVING, Rosehill Hospital, Hitchin
    Road (01462 678804)

ACCIDENT AND EMERGENCY

LISTER HOSPITAL, Coreys Mills Lane, Stevenage (01438 314333)

DAY HOSPITAL

ERNEST GARDINER DAY HOSPITAL, Pearsall Close (off Pixmore Avenue)
(01462 670955)

HOSPICE

GARDEN HOUSE HOSPICE, Gillison Close (off Pixmore Avenue) (01462 679540)

Public Bodies

LETCHWORTH GARDEN CITY COUNCIL (town council), 269 Icknield Way
(01462 682552; letchworthgardencity-council.org.uk),
NORTH HERTS DISTRICT COUNCIL Council Offices, Gernon Road
(01462 474000; www.north-herts.gov.uk)
LETCHWORTH GARDEN CITY HERITAGE FOUNDATION, Suite 401, The Spirella
Building, Bridge Road
(01462 476000; www.lgchf.com)
HERTS COUNTY COUNCIL County Hall, Pegs Lane, Hertford, SG13 8DE
(01438 737555; www. hertsdirect.org),
POLICE STATION, Nevells Road (0845 3300222)
POST OFFICES. The principal Post Office is at McColl's newsagents in Station
Road on the edge of the shopping area following the failure of a campaign
to halt the closure of the central Post Office in Broadway. There are sub
post offices on the Jackmans and Grange estates and at Norton (Green
Lane) and Willian.
TOURIST INFORMATION CENTRE, 33-35 Station Road. Provides a wide range of
tourist information both for Letchworth and elsewhere in the country. Is
also the centre for electric wheelchair provision under the Shopmobility
scheme. (01462 487868;
www.letchworthgc.com/contactus/touristinformationcentre.html).
PUBLIC LIBRARY, Broadway (01438 737333)

PART FOUR

Letchworth Walks

All these walks can be shortened, or taken in stages, by using the maps.

WALK 1 North East

(4 miles approx – allow 1 hr 45 min)

The **Railway Station** is a starting point for many visitors. Opened in 1912 to replace an earlier wooden structure located a few hundred yards to the west, it was designed with two island platforms so that tracks could be laid either side, giving four platforms in all. The outer two were, however, never built. Letchworth was planned around the railway, but the line is unobtrusive, passing through the town centre in a cutting.

COMMUTING IN LETCHWORTH

From the earliest days, people have commuted from Letchworth to London. Indeed, extra rush hour trains existed in the 1900s for people who settled in Letchworth but preferred to keep their jobs in the capital. Commuting really took hold after the electrification in 1977, which brought the fastest journey time to London down from 45 minutes to around 30 minutes. Now there are two trains per hour throughout the day to London, as well as many extra non-stop services at peak times that have standing room only.

In the days before Letchworth finally succumbed to the provision of pubs and bars in the town, the only pub in Letchworth was a train – the Cambridge Miniature Buffet Express, which ran every two hours through the day (and before the war was called the Garden Cities Buffet Express). When the last one ran, in 1977 on the eve of the new electric service, free party snacks were provided all the way to Cambridge.

The town's three main streets fan out from the station forecourt, Station Road to the left, then Leys Avenue, and Broadway diagonally to the right. Straight ahead between Leys Avenue and Broadway are *The Colonnade,* now the Hogshead pub, the Natwest Bank and the former Garden City offices, whose upper storeys are now flats.

◄ From the top of Spirella, a view of the restored gardens. Spirella once employed 2,000 people.

The starting point for Walk 1, Letchworth Garden City station opened in 1912 replacing an earlier, wooden building.

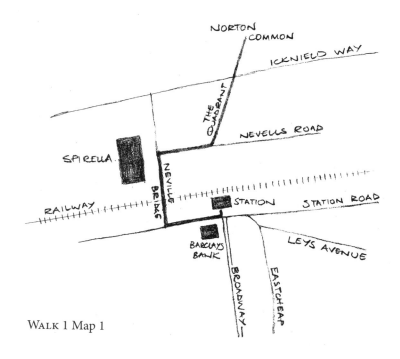

WALK 1 Map 1

Turn right, past the single storey Barclays Bank, the first of Letchworth's banks, built in 1908, and right again to recross the railway on **Neville Bridge,** named after the first chairman of First Garden City Limited, Sir Ralph Neville. Designed by Barry Parker, the bridge was completed only in 1930, and opened by the then Minister of Transport, Herbert Morrison. Plaques on each parapet commemorate the event. Prior to the opening of Neville Bridge, there was only a wooden footbridge, and vehicles had to cross the railway by the narrower Spring Road underbridge a quarter of a mile to the west.

As you come on to Neville Bridge the view is dominated by the gabled roofs of the **Spirella Building** on the left, the largest structure in Letchworth and an internationally important industrial building with a grade II* listing. Built between 1912 and 1921 to the design of local architect Cecil Hignett, this was the headquarters of a flourishing lingerie empire for around fifty years. It was founded by an American philanthropist William Wallace Kincaid (1868-1946), who, influenced by the Garden City movement, wanted to establish a new type of factory with enlightened employment practices, in what was then a green field site. But he also wanted his new factory to be the first thing visitors would see from the railway and refused to locate it in the planned industrial area. Such was the desire to bring Spirella – and its employment opportunities – into the town that he was allowed his chosen site.

Corsets having gone out of fashion, the factory – known as Castle Corset for reasons obvious when you look at it – closed in 1979. It has been restored by the Heritage Foundation at a cost of £11m and part of it serves as its head office. It also accommodates a number of other small and medium sized companies.

The full grandeur of the building can be appreciated from Nevells Road, including the restored gardens and fountains at the front. Better still, go round to the other side and look up at it from Bedford Road or from the car park to the west side. The Spirella was one of the first buildings to incorporate pre-stressed concrete, which has been used for most load bearing parts of the structure. The concrete has been painted cream to reduce the potential starkness of this material. It is also offset by the brick cladding, the wide glass windows, and above all by the tiled roof, now a common design feature even of factories and supermarkets but most unusual for an industrial building of that era. The building is open to the public during office hours – you can go in and use the ground floor cafe; from time to time tours of the building are given, which take in the splendid art nouveau ballroom on the top floor and the roof, where sunbathing was allowed.

SPIRELLA

The factory made corsets of a once revolutionary design, the garments being stiffened with wire springs rather than the traditional bone. This made them much more comfortable.

At its height, 2,000 people worked at Spirella, mostly female corsetières. They enjoyed baths, hairdressers and stylists, eye tests, capes to take home if it was raining, and repair facilities for their bicycles. Sunbathing was allowed on the roof in fine weather. A number of social events were provided in the ballroom during the evenings. From the memories recorded by Heather Elliott and John Sanderson in *Letchworth Recollections*, we can imagine that the inter-war workforce was highly motivated and that the company played a central part in the lives both of the employees and also of the town in general. 'You used to be able to have a bath once a week...and you were supplied with towels and soap. Then not every house had a bath especially in the villages.' 'At 21, I went to Spirella and stayed there for 21 years. It was a wonderful and lovely place to work for...If you were ill, you used to have milk drinks for a fortnight. We had health and beauty classes. We used to have black satin trousers and white satin tops, that was lovely.'

Looking at the Spirella building from Nevells Road, between the police station and the anonymous telephone exchange building, we are on the site of **The Sheds,** the earliest buildings in Letchworth, but long since demolished. The Sheds were home to the construction workforce, and resembled an army barracks. They served as dormitories, cookhouses, mess facilities and stores. The Spirella company started its activities in The Sheds in 1910, before the permanent factory was built.

As the construction workers either returned to London or found their own homes in the new city, other public uses were found for them, notably the first school in the Garden City, founded in November 1905.

Turn down **Nevells Road** (not connected with Sir Ralph Neville). This was formerly Exhibition Road and was one of the sites of the 1905 Cheap Cottages Exhibition. Many of these cottages still stand today. Turn left into **The Quadrant,** which continues on the same main southwest-northeast axis of the town

Spirella's founder was persuaded to come to Letchworth only if his factory was one of the first sights to greet visitors. Today it houses a multitude of enterprises, including the Garden City Heritage Foundation.

Weather-boarded cottage in The Quadrant, built for the 1905 Cheap Cottage Exhibition.

Workers' cottages are grouped round a green at Westholm, designed for Garden City Tenants by Parker and Unwin in 1906.

81

as Broadway, the other side of the railway station. On both sides, then along **Icknield Way**, are many unique designs of cottage, all built for £105 or less in 1905. **No 221 Icknield Way** is much photographed – a timber framed weather-boarded cottage designed by Bennett and Bidwell it came second in its class. **No 8 The Quadrant**, another entry, also employs weatherboarding, while **No 6** was built by the Bournville Village Trust, witnessing to the link with other urban developments of the time.

CHEAP COTTAGES EXHIBITION

The Cheap Cottages Exhibition of 1905 was the brainchild of the company secretary, Thomas Adams, who saw the scheme as a way of attracting builders and architects to the Garden City and also of bringing newcomers to Letchworth and putting the town on the map. A special day return fare from London of 3s 5d (17p) was charged and thousands of visitors made their way to the town in the summer of 1905.

Prizes were given for a number of categories of houses. Houses had to be built for less than £150. This would allow rents labourers could afford – the target being between 4s 6d and 5s 6d per week (23p-28p).

It allowed the builders the opportunity to experiment with different construction techniques. One (158 Wilbury Road) was built with prefabricated sections in less than 36 hours, while another, 4 Cross Street, had its concrete sections manu-factured on site. Some were steel framed, and one was round (140 Wilbury Road, now sadly demolished).

Cheap cottage exhibition houses can be seen in the Nevells Road and Icknield Way area, Wilbury Road, and also in Birds Hill. However, the winners of the group category, by Geoffry Lucas, are the ploughmen's cottages in Paddock Close, on the south side of the town – see Walk 3.

Two years later, in 1907, the company held a second exhibi-tion, this time an Urban Cottages Exhibition, repeating the ex-periment though with less success in terms of visitor numbers. The site of this second exhibition was predominantly in Lytton Avenue and Pixmore Way.

Though no further exhibitions of this type took place, the

tradition carried on in the form of the Daily Mail Ideal Homes
Exhibition. Lord Northcliffe, proprietor of that newspaper,
was a major supporter of Letchworth's housing experiments.

This walk will take in further sections of the exhibition area on the way back.
Meanwhile from The Quadrant, cross Icknield Way and take the straight path
across **Norton Common**. **Icknield Way** is one of the oldest routes in Britain, a
drove road that takes its name from the pre-Roman Iceni tribe and runs from
Suffolk to Berkshire along the line of the Chilterns. The present street follows
one of its likely courses (the old route probably consisted of several parallel
tracks) and, though at this point it bears little resemblance to the ancient track,
the enthusiastic walker can enjoy a more rural aspect of the Way to the east and
west of Letchworth, since the Icknield Way is now a long distance path.

This part of Norton Common, with its avenue of chestnut trees, has been
cultivated. To our left and ahead to the right is undisturbed woodland. Take
the straight path downhill (the path to the right leads towards the public tennis
courts, a bowling green and putting green as well as a play area for children).
At the foot of the hill, the wide grassy area has been used for a fair and firework
display on the town's Foundation Day.

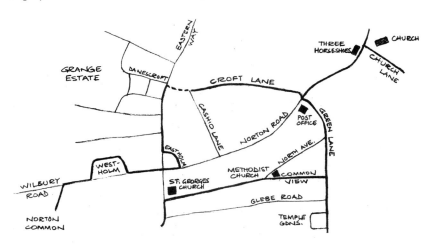

Walk 1 Map 2

A green lung in the middle of the Garden City: Norton Common abounds with wildlife and has the Pix brook running through it.

Technologically advanced, this 1905 Cheap Cottage Exhibition entry at 158 Wilbury Road used pre-cast materials and took 36 hours to erect. It was the work of John Brodie, Liverpool's City Engineer.

At the top of the hill at the far side of Norton Common, turn right into **Wilbury Road**, location of other Exhibition cottages. **No 158,** almost opposite, is particularly well known as a flat roofed concrete construction, designed by the City Engineer of Liverpool, JA Brodie. It is a sectional building and took 36 hours to erect. Not quite art deco in style, it could yet be from the 1920s rather than from 1905. Wilbury Road soon opens out on the left into **Westholm**, which was started in 1906, perhaps one of the best examples of a 'village green' in Letchworth, with original Parker and Unwin cottages all around. Note the typical gables and dormer windows, and the groupings into fours and sixes. Further along, turn left into **Eastholm**, which slightly predates Westholm and is very similar but is now cut through by Eastern Way. Follow Eastern Way, leading into the **Grange Estate**.

This London County Council overspill estate is 1940s council housing, but its layout follows Garden City design principles in creating open space and arranging houses in groups and the roads in gentle curves rather than straight lines, so that a more attractive and restful urban environment is achieved. The principal architect was Courtenay Crickmer, who had been involved in the Garden City from the early days, and it is interesting to see how times had moved on from the 1900s. True the houses are of much simpler design, without the gables, dormers and mock Tudor chimneys but, at the time it was built, this housing was considered progressive and good value, not least by the tenants, who were well prepared to tolerate the simpler designs.

The Grange Estate has its own shopping parade in Southfields, a pub, The Pelican, of 1960s post-teetotal origin, and a **Baptist Church** in Danescroft, built in 1963 and designed by Crickmer, then in his eighties, in association with W. Knott. There are extensive playing fields off Gaunts Way, overlooking the open country to the north.

Turn right opposite Danescroft, by a bus stop, down a small lane that leads to the corner of Croft Lane and Cashio Lane. These are part of the ancient village of Norton and predate the Garden City by many years; however there are many original garden city houses along both, as well as older and newer types. Of particular interest are a group by the Hitchin architect Geoffry Lucas: **No 3 Croft Lane**, '**Brierley**', a luxurious middle class home; and next door **Nos 5-7**, '**Dormer Cottages**', more modest but quite charming. No 7 has been sympathetically extended.

Opposite, on the corner of the two lanes, is '**Croft Corner**' by Cecil Hignett, architect of the Spirella Building – providing a contrast in scale and style. This is a three-storey structure and boasts a thatched roof, which was unusual for the

Cecil Hignett, the Spirella architect, designed Three Gables in Croft Lane as his own house.

St Nicholas, Norton, a quiet village church standing for nearly 800 years before the parish became part of the new Garden City.

Beating the ban: in the early days, Letchworth's only licensed premises were on the outskirts, such as The Three Horseshoes in Norton.

Garden City, though not for Norton and Croft Lane. The fall of the roof is so deep that the effect is almost of a pyramid. Hignett built his own house, 'Three Gables', a few yards away at **No 12 Croft Lane**. It also has low roofs to the front; the three gables are on the rear aspect.

Proceed along Croft Lane in the direction of Norton, passing the pond and the extension to the Greenway at the junction with Norton Road, and turn left. Further along on the right, the modern black buildings are converted barns. On the left-hand side of the road is the **Three Horseshoes** pub. Almost facing it are the village school, now much extended since its Victorian foundation, and, across Church Lane, the ancient parish church of **St Nicholas**. This is the heart of the old village of Norton. In **St Nicholas churchyard**, take the path diagonally right through the gravestones, with the church on your left, to the gate at the far end. If you then look round to your left, you will notice four gravestones decorated with the black, gold and red Belgian tricolour.

These are the graves of the four Belgian soldiers we have met earlier in this book – Corporal Louis Ledoux and privates Alphonse Dumont, Denijs Thonissen and Sylvain Sortet. They met their deaths toward the end of the First World War, between December 1917 and June 1918.

BELGIANS IN LETCHWORTH

The soldiers and their families were members of the first wave of foreign immigrants into Letchworth in 1915, following the fall of their country. Predominantly, the Belgians came to live in the Campers Road area, which became dubbed Little Antwerp, though some were accommodated in the Glebe Road area. There were about 3,000 altogether. To help the war effort, two of their number, Jacques Kryn and his engineer colleague Raoul Lahy, started to build Letchworth's biggest factory in Dunhams Lane (planning permission from Hitchin RDC arrived a few days after work started) which became the Kryn and Lahy munitions works, making shells for the allied armies. It became part of the George Cohen engineering group and served as a munitions factory again in the Second World War.

Most of the refugees returned home at the end of the war, but Albert I, King of the Belgians, presented the town with an oak tree and a plaque, which can still be seen in Howard Park (see Walk 2).

Publisher's pleasure: this attractive grouping of homes at Temple Gardens was built by JM Dent, the publisher, for its staff.

Norton Post Office helps keep a village atmosphere alive.

The little Methodist church at North Avenue: its origins go back to the Norton Mission, with strong links with the internationally famous evangelist Gipsy Smith. He travelled the Icknield Way as a boy and preached here as an old man. There is a memorial to his parents, who are buried nearby.

From the churchyard the path leads on across the meadow towards Norton Bury, and you can extend this walk by adding on the signposted circular walk that brings you back into Norton Church Lane (see the section on the Greenway). Church Lane is a picturesque road with a handful of old cottages and, on the left, the **Old Vicarage**, at one time the home of Sid Stapleton, founder of Stapleton's Tyre Services, which is still active in the town. An inveterate opponent of the Garden City Corporation and the leasehold principle, Stapleton took pride in owning one of Letchworth's few freehold properties: the former Church-owned building did not form part of the holding of First Garden City or its successors. He was reputed to change his Rolls-Royce every two years, placing the order for the next one when he took delivery of the latest vehicle.

Retrace your steps back to **Norton Post Office**, and turn left down Green Lane which, with Spring Road, was one of two north-south routes on the original Garden City site.

We shall take the second turning on the right, **Common View** but, before doing so, continue slightly further down Green Lane to **Temple Gardens** lower down the hill on the right. These are two groups of houses on three sides of a square, again giving a communal effect, arranged round a green space. These were built by the publishers, JM Dent and Co, one of the first large companies to move from London to Letchworth, for their staff, to help them settle. Work was a five minute walk away, across the railway line. Features such as the arched doorways, together with a heavier overall look, mark them as late Victorian houses rather than Arts and Crafts.

Returning to Common View, you will see one of the prettiest rows in Letchworth. In Edwardian times, these dwellings were described as 'working class housing'. The feel is more of the street of an ancient country village than of a Victorian terrace. The cottages have small front gardens and are arranged in a gently curving row in groups of six with gaps between.

The walk down the road reveals another pleasant green on the right, including allotments, and more 'labourers' cottages' (so described on their commemorative plaques) all put up before the First World War. Some have been painted in non-original colours, pink and sky blue, but the effect is in keeping, since coloured wash is very common in this area of England. A concession to the late 20th century is that much of the garden area of the cottages has been sacrificed to garages, but this is fortunately out of our view.

Towards the triangle at the corner of North Avenue stands **North Avenue Methodist Church.** Unusually, it is built across the triangle rather than facing it; pride of place on the street corner instead goes to the mini market. Partly destroyed by arson in 1996, the church premises have been restored with the aid of a Heritage Foundation grant and are home to a number of community groups, including the Arcadians theatre group.

GIPSY SMITH

North Avenue Methodist Church, still sometimes known as 'The Mission', has its origins in the mission of the free churches to the Norton area of the developing Garden City in the 1900s. It has associations with the evangelist Gipsy (Rodney) Smith (1860-1947) who was a preacher of worldwide fame, a Billy Graham of his day, who first worked with the Salvation Army in London under Booth and then preached worldwide, spending much of his time in the United States. When Rodney was a child of five, his gipsy family camped on Icknield Way while his mother Mary nursed a sister who was sick with smallpox. Mary contracted the disease and died. She was buried outside Norton Parish churchyard, though a later extension to the churchyard has brought her grave within it. Gipsy Smith's father Cornelius, himself a preacher, is buried with her.

In January 1908 Gipsy Smith visited for a few days and led some thinly attended meetings (the winter weather was not encouraging) which nevertheless set the new mission on its way. Then in 1934, as an old man, he was invited back by the congregation to speak and to visit the building of the new hall, which he allowed to be dedicated to the memory of his parents, Mary and Cornelius.

Gipsy Smith was born in a caravan in Epping Forest and died in 1947 in a first class cabin on board the liner Queen Mary, as it approached New York.

Further groups of cottages follow, many with large oval plaques showing their architects, builders and dates. Parker and Unwin, Crickmer, Bennett and Bidwell and Hignett are all represented. Many are Housing Association properties, built by Letchworth Cottages and Buildings or the Howard Cottage Society. At Cromwell Green, the vista opens out into another open space. Then there follow some inter-war bungalows before Common View ends by the striking

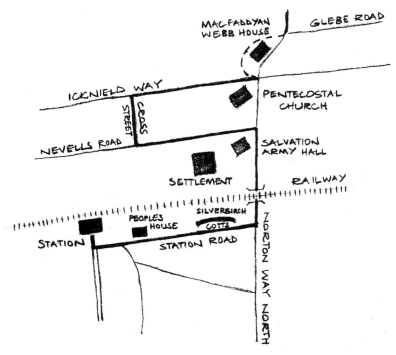

WALK 1 Map 3

white spire of the modern **St George's Church** on the corner on the right. The spire, which is formed of two acute triangles, appears to support the rest of the building. The Church Hall, in Common View, was the original church building.

Turn left by the church, back into **Norton Way North**. Opposite is a number of interesting early Garden City houses. Just to the right, **Nos 7-7A**, 'Elmwood Cottages' are by the master Arts and Crafts architect MH Baillie Scott. This was supposedly his entry in the cheap cottages exhibition but was disqualified for being well over budget at £420 for the pair. Baillie Scott was too perfectionist to compromise on his design, which was widely praised at the time for its romantic re-creation of the country cottage in a modern idiom. His own drawing envisaged a grassy, bushy frontage which is more romantic than the

Elmwood Cottages, Norton Way North: intended as a 1905 Cheap Cottages Exhibition entry by arts and crafts architect MH Baillie Scott.

The pub with no beer: The Skittles Inn in Nevells Road, by Parker and Unwin, 1906, caught the atmosphere of a traditional English pub – but with one vital ingredient missing. As Letchworth Settlement, it became a pioneering adult education centre and is still going strong.

present reality of the busy street. From the street we can admire the mediaeval style porch and doors, the mullioned windows and dormers and gables. Inside space was created by an open plan layout, complemented by plain wooden furnishings and an inglenook housing the cooking range. The exterior is not as pretty as it once was, the modern square extensions replacing the original swept-down roofs which came almost to ground level above a small, sunken scullery on each side. In the interests of practicality, subsequent owners have raised the sculleries to the main ground floor level.

The twin-gabled **No 13** is another by Geoffry Lucas, slightly more conservative but less 'rural'. **No 23** is one of the first flat roofed houses in the country, by Taperall and Haase, while **No 29** is another Baillie Scott mock Tudor example, with a complicated roof and chimney structure.

A slight diversion can be made into the south-eastern corner of Norton Common by taking the entrance opposite Glebe Road alongside **MacFadyen Webb House**. This sheltered housing development is named after a local doctor, Norman MacFadyen, and Nurse Webb who served at the Spirella Company and around the district. Continuing round the back of that building the 1935 open air swimming pool (open May half term to September) is reached. Rejoining the road at the corner of Icknield Way and Norton Way North, we find another corner dominated by a church building. This is the former **Elim Pentecostal Church** (now used by Letchworth Town Council as its base), designed by Hignett and built in 1925. Here turn right up Icknield Way as far as Cross Street, to re-enter the Exhibition cottages area. On the corner of Cross Street is an attractive bungalow, **No 2, 'Nook Cottage'**, now extended from its original compact quartered form, while **No 4 Cross Street** is one of the country's first concrete buildings, built from blocks made on site.

Re-entering **Nevells Road**, turn left. Almost opposite is the **Settlement**, the 'pub with no beer'. Built by Parker and Unwin in 1906, within walking distance from 'The Sheds', it was established as the Skittles Inn by the Quaker Edward Cadbury and the Welsh Baptist Aneurin Williams, who was to succeed Neville as chairman of the Company, to provide entertainment, food and non-alcoholic drink for Letchworth workers. The design, a Parker and Unwin classic, follows the traditional lines of an English country pub, with an open porch with bench seating and a cosy bar and inglenooks. There was a skittle alley, now converted into the Little Theatre, which contains a picture of Wallace Kincaid, founder of the Spirella Company. The Settlement is home to a number of local societies, including the local RSPB branch, the Camera Club, the Letchworth Garden City Society, and the Settlement Players theatre group. It is an important centre for adult education, offering a wide range of courses supervised by Cambridge University.

To the right of the Settlement, in the line of its car park, a lane used to run through the railway embankment to connect with Station Road the other side. This was the 'cattle creep' which, along with the Spring Road bridge and a level crossing at the end of Dunhams Lane, formed the only crossings of the railway at the foundation of the town. It was replaced by the Norton Way bridge when that was constructed in 1913, and no trace of it exists.

LETCHWORTH – A TEETOTAL TOWN

Although alcohol related problems are a frequent subject of public debate, it is still difficult for the modern mind to appreciate the strength of the temperance movement 100 years ago. Howard made two references to it in *Tomorrow* – one in the introduction, where he referred to alcohol as one of the current social problems, but a problem on which opinions were divided, and again in the section on semi-municipal enterprise, where he explicitly argued that a drinking ban would merely move the problem elsewhere. He was sure that the improved conditions of life in the Garden City would reduce alcoholism, and expected that 'the community would certainly take care to prevent the undue multiplication of licensed houses'.

Following a visit to the town by the British Women's Temperance Association, it was agreed that the town's attitude to the provision of licensed premises should be decided by popular vote, and a series of referendums continued to reject the sale of alcohol. It was eventually authorised at clubs such as the Conservative and Unionist Club and at Letchworth Hall Hotel, while brewers in Baldock did a steady trade delivering to Letchworth by horse-drawn drays. Eventually, the Railway allowed the sale of alcohol from premises it owned in the station forecourt, to the intense irritation of other local retailers who finally forced a decisive vote in favour of the sale of alcohol. This took place in 1958, and the immediate consequence was the building of the Broadway Hotel, which became the first town centre licensed premises.

Follow Nevells Road back to the bottom of the hill, turn right into Norton Way past the **Salvation Army Hall**, under the 1913 bridge – mind the pigeons! – and right again into **Station Road**. One of the first roads completed in the Garden City, the shops at its foot are among the earliest, while those at the top beyond the arcade were among the last, being finished in 1922 by Bennett and Bidwell. On the right, screened from the traffic by shrubbery, are more early cottages, **Silver Birch Cottages,** original Parker and Unwin of 1905-07, which were restored in 1980. At the top of the road, returning to the station, is the **People's House,** designed by Hignett, which took over from the Skittles Inn in 1924 as the town's main restaurant and meeting place. It is now the Job Centre.

Silver Birch Cottages, Station Road, by Parker and Unwin, 1905, form an attractive group set back from the road opposite the shops.

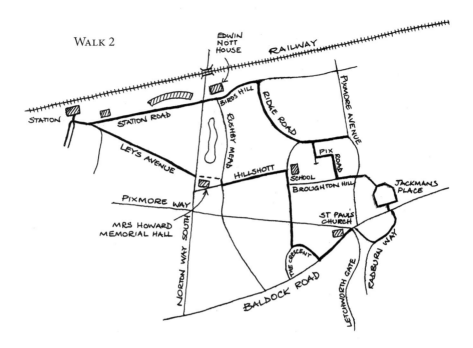

WALK 2

WALK 2 South East

(3 miles approx – allow 1 hr 20 min)

This walk takes in different ages of the Garden City enabling us to see the way it developed in stages from the 1900s to the 1960s and later. Examples of housing from different decades can be seen and we skirt the industrial estate close by.

From the station, proceed left down Station Road, described at the end of Walk one. Note the **People's House** on the left, and **Silver Birch Cottages.**

At the bottom of the road, cross the roundabout into **Birds Hill**, one of the first roads to be made up in the new Garden City. Glance to the right along **Rushby Mead**, which we shall visit on the way back. Both Rushby Mead and Birds Hill are excellent examples of the art of landscaping, which 100 years ago was a new concept for towns. We have crossed the line of the Pix brook, which at this point is in a tunnel, and Rushby Mead follows the line of the stream. This area of the town provides excellent examples of Unwin's ideas on grouping cottages at angles and in cul-de-sacs rather than in regimented rows.

The modern **Edwin Nott House**, on the left, is sheltered housing provided by the Howard Cottage Society.

Birds Hill bends elegantly up the contours of the hill. On the left are some well restored mansard roof houses. Mansarding is the use of tiles to form the walls of the upper storey. It is common, for example, in larger French châteaux, but a century ago was unusual for a small English house. It was an economy measure, saving bricks, and these houses, by the architect V Dunkerley, were entries in the 1905 Cheap Cottages Exhibition. Nearest to the road is a plaque on **No 14**, commemorating a civic award for their restoration. On the corner of Ridge Road are two groups of Parker and Unwin cottages, one facing down the hill and one facing north to Birds Hill, both using the contours to exaggerate the height of the hill, which in truth is no hill at all but a small rise.

Turn right into **Ridge Road**. One hundred yards along on the left is a particularly notable cul-de-sac of cottages, **Nos 20-66 Ridge Road**, with the feel of a rural lane. Sadly the 1970s chimneys of the power station give away the fact that the industrial estate is only a matter of yards away behind the belt of trees at the back. Further along, Ridge Road widens to give another village green effect (and the chimneys are better shielded by the tall limes at the rear). At the top, at **Pixmore Avenue**, the fringe of the industrial estate is reached.

On the corner at the left is a fine small industrial building designed by Parker and Unwin, originally the **Edmundsbury Weavers factory**, built in 1908. Opposite are the sites once occupied by two of Letchworth's first major companies, **Arden Press**, now commemorated in Arden Press Way, and, down the hill on the corner with Works Road, the old building used by **Dent's bookbinders**, which produced, among other things, the Everyman series. Along with the Garden City Press, this corner of town became an important centre for the printing industry.

Retracing your steps a few yards back down Ridge Road, turn left into **Pix Road**, a community within the community, known as the Pixmore Estate after the farm on which it was built. Pix Road has a less spacious layout than Rushby Mead, with a right-angled dog leg bend at its halfway point. It is the earliest Parker and Unwin attempt at grouping and landscaping, and the design of the houses is much less radical, using much local yellow Arlesey brick and more closely resembling the Victorian terraces that they were to replace. As is im-

The so-called Noah's Ark cottages in Birds Hill, another entry in the 1905 Cheap Cottages Exhibition, by V Dunkerley.

Parker and Unwin cottages in Ridge Road, 1906, on the way to the industrial area. A buffer zone separated the houses from the industry.

More clever landscaping, this time in Rushby Mead, developed in 1911-12 for the Howard Cottage Society.

mediately apparent, Pix Road was not designed for the car – it was for walking or cycling – and remains an intriguing quiet corner.

Turn left at the end of Pix Road into **Broughton Hill**. Opposite is **Boscombe Court,** a group of flats built by the Howard Cottage Society and opened in 1973, which replaced 32 original cottages in what was Dimsdale Place and which were beyond saving. Cross Pixmore Avenue into **Jackmans Place,** constructed in 1919-21 to designs by Bennett and Bidwell, and the contrast with Pix Road is very evident. The use of culs-de-sac and grouping of the houses is much more sophisticated. Observe in particular the way in which houses in the first group are set at angles to each other rounding the corner, and, at the first junction, the group on the left which turn the angle so neatly. Front doors are arranged with some forward facing and others side facing to add to privacy. These houses were developed from designs for Rushby Mead, but are more austere due to the inflation of building costs after the Great War. They were the first houses built after the First World War by the newly formed Letchworth Urban District Council and, like other Letchworth designs, the houses and their little estate became a model for elsewhere across the country.

Jackmans Place leads into Baldock Road; turn left, over the pelican crossing and right, by the modern petrol station, into **Radburn Way,** the lasso-shaped main feeder road of the 1960s Jackmans Estate, which represents yet another generation of town planning. Here we are about to enter postwar London over-spill housing, built by the UDC to a design by the Letchworth architect William Barnes in conjunction with London County Council, which provided much of the funding.

The name Radburn has a particular significance, commemorating the export of the Garden City ideal to America. Radburn was built as a new town near New York in 1928 and laid out complete with 'Howard Drive'. It was particularly innovative for its day, in that it was geared to the needs of the car and, for the first time, had pedestrian routes separated from the motor roads. This is the style that has been incorporated in the Jackmans Estate, America's return gift to Letchworth, and is also an important feature in the design of Stevenage and other postwar new towns.

'Town-country' 1960s style, viewing the open spaces of the Jackmans estate, can be experienced by continuing the walk to the left, down Quinn Way and Webb Close. These are 1980s developments on the site of the former Willian comprehensive school. At the end of Webb Close, take the path across the field to the houses. Turn sharp right on to the tarmac path at the back of the houses and follow it gently downhill, straight on across the green. Follow the diagonal

Early housing by the Letchworth Urban District Council in Jackmans Place, 1919, to designs by Bennett and Bidwell.

Pixmore Way is the site of several entries in the 1907 Urban Cottages Exhibition, along with some large individual homes and 1920s Letchworth Urban District Council housing designed by CM Crickmer and Allen Foxley.

line through the housing, past the concrete mushroom, then bear right again between two rows of houses and follow the path under a subway, which is Radburn Way.

The path continues round the back of Freeman House out of the estate and emerges near the roundabout into Baldock Road adjacent to **St Paul's Church.** St Paul's was a 'Victory Church' built after the First World War. It was never fully completed at its east end and the present porch is a recent addition.

With the church on your right, go along **Baldock Road**. To your right are **Pixmore Cottages,** which bear a date plaque of 1868. These picturesque semi-detached houses are the only pre-1903 buildings in the area of the Garden City between old Letchworth and Norton villages.

Turn right into **The Crescent** and descend back to **Pixmore Way**. This area is all UDC housing of the 1920s, built to designs by Crickmer and Foxley. Though The Crescent is a swirl of pleasing bends, Pixmore Way is an important approach avenue to the town centre and Crickmer believed a straighter line of housing was appropriate.

HOMES FIT FOR HEROES

Towards the end of the First World War, Lloyd George's government committed itself to a programme of housebuilding under the slogan 'Homes fit for heroes'. For the first time, local authorities were given the power to build subsidised housing. This followed strenuous advocacy on the part of Raymond Unwin, who wanted to expand the availability of working class housing on the Garden City low-density model. From 1919, Letchworth Urban District Council, first elected that April, took a greater initiative in housebuilding than the First Garden City Company, unsurprisingly as it had access to the subsidies and to cheaper borrowing facilities. It was also ready with its plan, developed from the Parker and Unwin layout.

The new houses are plainer than the pre-war designs, deliberately so as the Ministry of Health, which still sponsored housing, insisted on economy, with no fancy dormers and gables. However, contemporaries such as Charles Purdom considered them better value for money than the pre-war designs, especially since they were more spacious.

Cross Pixmore Way into **Ridge Avenue**, which is all pre-First World War Howard Cottage Society housing in an attractive uniform cream and green. On the right, Bennetts Close, with its iron railings, is the site of the former Pixmore school, which is now in Rushby Mead. Further along, **Hillshott Infants School** was formerly the Pixmore Institute, an important social centre for early residents, where lectures and public meetings were held.

Turn left into Hillshott, then continue to the junction of **Rushby Mead,** where we are in a much praised semi-urban landscape with the park opposite. Before turning right, look the other way to the southward continuation of Rushby Mead and note the angles in the street and the arrangement of the houses. Rushby Mead was started in 1911 and for the time this was a revolutionary piece of landscaping, with the lane reflecting the meandering course of the Pix brook. The buildings are variously by Parker and Unwin, Bennett and Bidwell, and Crickmer, and financed by the Howard Cottage Society, which still owns the majority. The livery of cream rendering and green woodwork, which is original, adds to the unity of the estate.

HOWARD COTTAGE SOCIETY

Formed in 1911 to promote affordable housing, the Howard Cottage Society (HCS), which is a housing association, has been an important part of Letchworth life since its inception. Many of its Directors and senior staff, and, at first, its offices, have been shared with First Garden City Limited. It currently owns over 1,250 rented homes, mostly in Letchworth but now more and more in towns and villages within a 20-mile radius.

Before 1916 it built 395 homes, of which Rushby Mead is the most well known development, distinguished by the cream and green livery of the houses. After the First World War the fortunes of the Society ebbed and flowed as housing associations tended to go in and out of fashion with central government. Between 1919 and 1974 the majority of new building was carried out by the local authority. But the 1974 and 1988 Housing Acts created a much more favourable climate for housing associations and the Howard Cottage Society is now expanding and very active, particularly in the provision of sheltered accommodation.

Apart from Rushby Mead, it owns Meadow Way Court (see

walk three) and has extensive properties in Archers Way and Monklands (1930s developments), the Grange Estate (1940s) and some interesting 1948 bungalows, Corner Close, at the junction of Bedford Road and Redwoods Way. The biggest recent development, Valley Road, which took Howard Cottage Society's housing to over 1,000, was opened by the Queen in July 1993.

Cross **Howard Park** by the path to the left opposite Rushby Walk, past the lake to Norton Way South, noting on the left the plaque and the oak tree presented by the King of Belgium in recognition of Letchworth's assistance to its refugees during the First World War. On the left is the restored **Mrs Howard Memorial Hall,** an intimate rather than a grand public hall, Letchworth's first, opened in 1906 in memory of Ebenezer Howard's first wife Elizabeth. The intimacy is achieved by the typical Arts and Crafts devices of its low roof, dormer windows and modest front entrance porch. It has recently been extended, widening the scope of the facilities on offer. A number of organisations are to take responsibility for running it.

Turn right to return up **Leys Avenue**, one of the main shopping streets. Note the gentle curve up the hill. The buildings at the top on the left (WH Smith) were once the temperance hotel, while those on the right, including the covered Arcade, were the last to be built, in 1922 by Bennett and Bidwell. Finish your walk in any one of the numerous cafés, restaurants or pubs

Space to breathe: Howard Park on the edge of the town centre, with its paddling pool, playground and extensive grass area for games, is a summer favourite with small children.

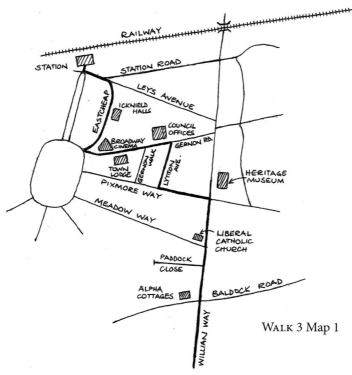

WALK 3 Map 1

WALK 3 South West

(3 miles approx – allow 1 hr 30 min)

This walk takes us through some of the most elegant parts of Arts and Crafts Letchworth.

Starting from Station Place, go up **Eastcheap,** one of the town's main shopping streets. On the left, above the first group of shops, are the **Icknield Halls,** while further along at approximately the entrance to the new Commerce Way was the site of the original Fire Station. Then, on the site now occupied by Poundstretcher, was the first of the town's two cinemas, the **Palace,** one of the earliest in the country, built in 1909. With the boom in cinema following the introduction of the talkies, the second much larger cinema, the **Broadway**, was opened in 1936. Originally also provided with a stage for live performances, it is a typical inter-war art deco monument, designed by Letchworth architect Wilson Bidwell, and has been restored to its original splendour by the Heritage Foundation.

The shopping parade on the right of Eastcheap is relatively modern, having been built in the 1960s with the awnings added in the 1980s. Prior to that there was a grassy open space, awaiting development, known as *The Arena*. What remains, opposite the cinema, is now a car park. Substantial redevelopment is planned here by the Heritage Foundation

Turning left round the corner at the Broadway Cinema into Gernon Road, passing the 1960s shopping development on the left. On the right is **Town Lodge,** (Hignett, 1923) which is an administrative office for North Herts District Council. Take a short detour to the right down Gernon Walk to discover two buildings which encapsulate Letchworth's religious diversity, with the **Sikh Temple** on the left and the flat roofed **Vasanta Hall** on the right, Letchworth's meeting place for the Theosophical Society and now a Spiritualist church.

Return to Gernon Road, passing the new Council Office block on the left, of which Miller says with polite understatement: 'The over vivid red brickwork and dark brown glass panels contrast uneasily with the small scale of the housing opposite.' Take the next right turn into **Lytton Avenue**. This is the site of the second Cottage Exhibition of 1907, this time redesignated the 'Urban Cottages Exhibition'. There are a number of picturesque cottages and **Nos 7-17** on the right moving away from the town, by Crickmer, are particularly notable, set back from the lane across a green. Turning left at Pixmore Way, we pass the winners of that competition, **Nos 110-120 Pixmore Way**, also built by Crickmer.

Another short diversion to the left at the roundabout with Norton Way South brings us to the **Garden City Heritage Museum,** offices of the Parker and Unwin partnership. The right hand section of the building, with its thatched roof, is a later extension by Parker to provide living accommodation for himself and his family.

HERITAGE MUSEUM

The building was left as a legacy to the town by Mrs Barry Parker. Opened as a museum in 1973, its remit covers all

Communal living was an early Letchworth theme. These homes in Meadow Way, 1916 and 1924-25, were designed by Courtenay Crickmer and intended specifically for business women.

Melverley in Pixmore Way, 1910, was the home of Alex Maclean, immortalised by the Macleans toothpaste brand.

The home of Courtenay Crickmer in Baldock Road, built to his own design.

aspects of the Garden City movement. It has periodic special displays on Garden City themes while the permanent exhibits include the drawing office and Barry Parker's office, kept in Arts and Crafts original style. In the garden outside is a millennium time capsule buried by Letchworth schoolchildren.

Since the establishment of the Heritage Museum, the Town Museum and Art Gallery on Broadway Gardens has continued to display all local non-Garden City related items, archaeology and natural history, together with a regular series of art exhibitions.

Back on the corner of Pixmore Way are more interesting buildings. The Central Methodist Church of 1914 is most prominent on the south west angle of the roundabout. Opposite it, hiding behind a thicker screen of shrubbery, is **Abendheim,** a mock Bavarian chalet designed by another prominent Garden City architect, Harold Clapham Lander. To its left in Pixmore Way is **Melverley,** a large house with a Tudor style doorway, designed by an estate agent named Underwood and once home of the first sales manger of the Spirella Company, Alex Maclean, who later set up his own business making 'own brand' products for chemists. His name lives on in Macleans toothpaste. In the 1920s Melverley became the home of the Shelvoke family, who founded the well-known firm of Shelvoke and Drewry, manufacturers of dustcarts. Melverley's grounds were once much more extensive but have been built on to form **Robert Humbert House,** a residential home round the next corner in Rushby Mead.

Returning to Norton Way South and continuing in a southerly direction toward the traffic lights at the junction with Baldock Road, there is a small church on the corner of Meadow Way, **St Alban's Liberal Catholic,** another Letchworth religious curiosity. It has weatherboarding round its little porch, and rendered walls. As well as being home to independent Catholic worshippers, it also hosts a high Anglican congregation. True to Garden City tradition, the congregation has maintained an attractive allotment garden in the grounds.

Further along on the right, **Paddock Close** has some early cottages. Those on the right, **Nos 1-4** and **5-8,** were winners of their group in the 1905 Cheap Cottages Exhibition. They were designed by Geoffry Lucas.

The last end terrace house in Norton Way South, **No 361,** bears a commemorative plaque noting that Ebenezer Howard lived here (between 1903 and 1911). Round the corner on the right in Baldock Road are **Alpha Cottages,** the first buildings put up in the new Garden City in 1904. Built by a local Hitchin firm,

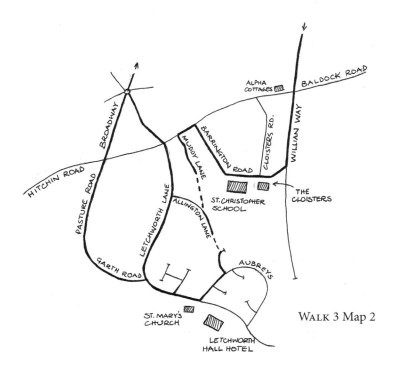

WALK 3 Map 2

Picton and Hope, before Parker and Unwin's appointment as architects to the Company, the style was disapproved of by the new team.

Crossing at the traffic lights and walking up **Willian Way**, the striking house on the right, **No 7**, was the home of Letchworth architect Wilson Bidwell, its rear shielded by a wall running the width of the plot. Continue up Willian Way to the next junction and turn right into **Barrington Road**. On the left is the extraordinary **Cloisters**, with its turrets, balconies and spiral staircases. Legend has it that its form was seen in a dream by its founder, Annie Lawrence. It was built in 1906 to the design of W H Cowlishaw. Annie Lawrence's vision and life in The Cloisters have been described earlier in this book. The building's interior and grounds have been much altered since Annie Lawrence's day and since 1948 have been owned by the Freemasons.

Past The Cloisters, we come to the buildings of St Christopher School, one of Letchworth's first and an important progressive independent school serving the area. The original building, which is behind others on the left as we walk through, is by Crickmer and dates from 1909. St Christopher School took over the building from the original occupants, the first Letchworth School, in 1928 when it moved from its original buildings in Broadway.

Bearing right after going through two cycle barriers, we pass the preparatory school on the right to rejoin Baldock Road. Turn left, then left again after 100 yards into Muddy Lane, to reach the site of the opening ceremony of the Garden City, held in a marquee on a sea of mud after pouring rain on October 9 1903. In Muddy Lane on the right is **Arunside**, now part of St Christopher but originally a pair of semi-detached houses occupied by the Unwins and the Parkers. Parker extended his half by adding a sleeping balcony and a third floor. Opposite on the other side of Muddy Lane are the modern buildings and courts of Letchworth Tennis Club. Muddy Lane becomes a footpath straight ahead, the old right of way known as the Alington Path which has been kept through the Manor Park Estate and can be walked all the way to Willian. On the right is another St Christopher boarding house, Arunwood, which was the Rectory. Among its occupants was Lord Olivier, the actor, whose father was rector of Letchworth. Follow this path to the first close of new houses and bear right into this close – a 1970s development, but unusual in that its name – Chaomans – is a typing mistake. The close should have been called Chapmans but the name was misread.

Turning right down the hill, join Letchworth Lane in the original village of Letchworth, now represented by a row of 17th century cottages, the tiny old **church of St Mary**, which dates from the 12th century, the **golf club** to the right and the **Letchworth Hall Hotel** beyond the church on the left, which has been heavily extended from the original 15th century manor house. It became a hotel in 1904 to cater for visitors to the new Garden City. At that time, the population of the parish of Letchworth was a mere 91. Both Willian and Norton were bigger.

The walk turns right and returns to Baldock Road, either by following Letchworth Lane or taking the left hand turn at the bottom of the hill and up Garth Road, then through a connecting path into Pasture Road. This whole triangular area is filled with attractive and nowadays well-shielded architect designed housing. Notable examples are **Glaed Hame** off Pasture Road, built by Parker and Unwin for Howard Pearsall, a director of FGC Limited, **Nos 16-18 Baldock Road** by Bennett and Bidwell, Bennett's first Garden City home, and **Nos 35-37 Baldock Road** by Lander. Crickmer designed and lived in **Nos 15-17**

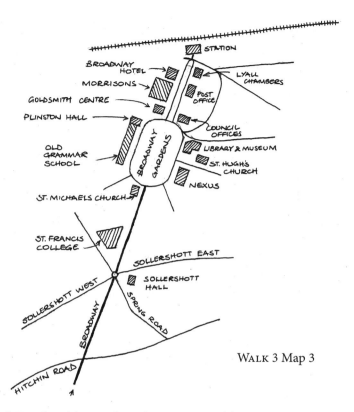

WALK 3 Map 3

Baldock Road and his work is also represented by **Arana** and **Crossways** in **Hitchin Road**, as Baldock Road is renamed as it draws closer to Hitchin, and **Dean Row** in **Pasture Road**. **Corrie Wood** in Hitchin Road was MH Baillie Scott's last Letchworth House.

Head back down **Broadway**, the town's main axis on the original plan. On the right are two houses featuring the typical upstairs sleeping balconies, with **No 508**, by Foxley, a fine example. At Sollershott Circus, the roundabout where Sollershott East, Sollershott West and Spring Road join Broadway, **Carfax** on the left is by Bennett and Bidwell, designed on the 'butterfly' plan to maximise sunlight.

The carriageway on this part of Broadway is off centre. This is because in the original plans there was to have been a tramway linking the new town with Hitchin. Sollershott Circus itself is claimed as the first roundabout in the country, an idea imported by Howard from Chicago. Serving three intersecting routes, it eventually proved to be an ideal traffic regulation system; however it was some years before either horse drawn or motorised traffic got the idea of circulating in a clockwise direction only!

A short detour down leafy **Sollershott West** reveals more graceful houses. A favourite is Baillie Scott's masterpiece at **No 17**, Tanglewood, not a large house but a beautiful example of arts and crafts at its best. Built in a hall style, it has a spacious interior.

Back on the south east corner of Sollershott Circus is **Sollershott Hall,** a Howardian attempt at communal living and now private flats. This consisted originally of 32 flats and has since been extended, not particularly sympathetically.

COMMUNAL LIVING

One Edwardian idea of an alternative lifestyle was that of communal living, which had a practical benefit since the intention was that people of middle to lower incomes who could not afford servants could in effect share them. Cooking, laundry etc were done communally by shared staff. Howard himself lived in Sollershott Hall from 1912 to 1920.

The other example of communal dwellings in Letchworth is in Meadow Way, arranged round a green either side of the road. These were designed for professional women and were built by the Howard Cottage Society.

Hampstead Garden Suburb displays similar courtyard style accommodation by Lucas, Baillie Scott and others. The communal living ideal has lost out to the modern preference for privacy. The constraint of being tied to fixed dining times, together with advances in domestic science that made self-catering more attractive, led to its extinction by World War Two at Sollershott Hall, though it lasted until 1972 at Meadow Way. Both at Sollershott Hall and Meadow Way, the common rooms were converted into extra flats.

Looking up Broadway to the town centre, this is the main Parker and Unwin thoroughfare for the city. Despite being a main axis, it was far from the first

Sollershott West, a broad, leafy road of large houses by several of the Garden City's principal architects. At its end is what is reputed to be Britain's first roundabout.

Letchworth Library was designed by Courtenay Crickmer and dates from 1938; the adjacent Museum and Art Gallery, 1914-20, is by Barry Parker. Both were extended to designs by Crickmer in 1962.

The Post Office building in Broadway is from 1912 and the work of Bennett and Bidwell. The Post Office itself has, sadly, moved to far less appropriate premises.

area to be constructed, being developed in the 1920s when the Garden City had already been in existence for about 20 years. In the early days, this was therefore all green fields nearly as far as the station. Then the cinder path was metalled and the fine Georgian style houses on the right were put up. The adoption of the Georgian style, after so much Arts and Crafts vernacular, was no doubt influenced by the use of Georgian and Queen Anne styles by Lutyens at Hampstead, where Unwin had been playing a leading role. On the left, the buildings of the independent girls' school, **St Francis' College**, are the dominant feature. The first Italian-style buildings nearest the circus are the original St Christopher School (see above), started in 1919 by the Theosophist luminary Mrs Annie Besant and featuring balconies for outdoor teaching, and these facilities have been expanded by the addition of the 1930s buildings that form the core of the school today.

Broadway Gardens provide an airy welcome to the town centre, and were completely remodelled for the centenary in 2003. The 17-jet fountain at the south end provides a splendid focal point. All that is left of the original trees are the three oaks at the north end, which Parker and Unwin used as the focal point of their plan and the alignment for this main axis.

Clockwise round the Gardens, the buildings are **St Michael's Church,** high Anglican, which replaced the former, and always temporary, parish church in Norton Way South in the late 1960s. It contains some attractive modern stained glass by John Hayward. The architect was Laurence King. Then the **Old Grammar School,** designed by Parker in the 1930s, which is now a home for various local government departments and voluntary organisations. Then **Plinston Hall,** which is Letchworth's principal theatre, concert hall and meeting place, converted from the Grammar School Hall. It is a convertible hall with retractable tiered seating allowing it to be used as a theatre or for a variety of other functions.

The north-west corner of the gardens spent nearly 100 years as something of a problem area. In the original plan, this should have formed the entrance to Westcheap a further shopping street to balance Eastcheap the other side of Broadway, but financial stringencies meant this never happened. In the 1960s the site was taken by North Herts Technical College, which was accommodated in a series of flat roofed prefabricated buildings typical of that era and, though it was a welcome facility for the town's young people, the buildings were unloved. All this was swept aside in the 1990s with the college now represented by the **Goldsmith's** building on the corner, and **Morrison's** supermarket behind, both opened in 1999 as an important part of the town centre's regeneration.

Next come the **Council Offices** of 1935 (Bennett and Bidwell) with the attractive clock tower, very typical of the period; the **Library,** (Crickmer, 1938) in a more modern style; and the earliest of the group, the **Museum,** (Parker, 1914-1920). **St Hugh of Lincoln** Roman Catholic Church is a 1960s building, replacing what is now its Church Hall just down Pixmore Way. Finally we come to the largest office block in Letchworth, the **Nexus Building,** a brave and partly successful attempt to improve what had been a dreadful 1960s eyesore, the ICL headquarters. Reclad with its glass fronting and topped by an unusual dome, the Nexus Building has become a new landmark for the town centre.

Before leaving the Broadway Gardens we should note some of the monuments that they contain. By the Nexus Building is the **John F. Kennedy Memorial,** which serves as a reminder that these were named the Kennedy Gardens between 1963 and 2003. In the centre, on the paved area, is a low relief plaque showing Unwin's 1912 proposal for the square, featuring a grand church and public buildings, while in the two northern corners are new bowers that shelter similar plaques of Parker and of Unwin.

TOWN SQUARE – UNACHIEVED AMBITIONS?

A Central town square was a feature of all three designs for the Garden City, not only Parker and Unwin's, and Howard's own circular layout proposed a central circus with grand public buildings and concentric boulevards. The difficulty in developing these lay in the fact that funding for these facilities had to come from the rents from housing and industry, and so long as, in the early days, these remained sluggish, the monumental architecture had to be delayed. In Letchworth, it was never completed. At Welwyn Garden City, the plan was more successfully executed.

The plans for the central square have always proved over-ambitious. It is probably the case that the town square is more suited to a town of 100,000 people than 30,000. It is as big as any square in London including Trafalgar Square, and compares with any in Paris or other great continental cities. Therefore, while it is a precious open space, it is always likely to lack the bustle of squares in a larger city. A modern town of Letchworth's size could not support the amount of retail, residential and restaurant development necessary around its perimeter for it to become the true centre of gravity of the town.

The same comments could equally be made of the contemporary central square at Hampstead Garden Suburb, which contains two large churches and an institute (now a school) but which lacks animation because of its lack of shops and restaurants.

Passing between the oaks we complete the tour along the boulevard section of Broadway, which has changed extensively in recent years. The central area has been replanted and currently affords a view of the whole street. The new college and supermarket are on the site of the old Primitive Methodist Church, 1914, which had a fine broad colonnaded front. A bust of Ebenezer Howard marks the spot. Morrison's new building has retained the frontage of Parker's **Boys Club** and the **Magistrates Court,** while finally on the left there is the **Broadway Hotel,** Letchworth's first licensed public bar, opened in 1961 after a referendum finally agreed, after over 50 years, to allow the sale of alcohol in the town.

On the right, as we have already noted, the parade of shops is a 1960s addition on the grassy arena, then comes the **Post Office** building and finally the former Garden City offices, now converted into flats as **Lyall Chambers**.

THE LETCHWORTH COUNTRYSIDE and beyond

Built as a town merging with the country, Letchworth has always valued its open spaces. Although the agricultural land owned by the farms – Pixmore and Wilbury – soon succumbed to the developers, two important 'green lungs' were retained in the centre of the new housing. Howard Park, along the Pix brook, was kept as a landscape feature and Rushby Mead, which runs along its eastern edge, is an early example of the retention of the natural contours in the layout of the road. Howard Park has since been developed as a recreational area, with a popular children's play area and paddling pool. Adjacent to it is Howard Garden, the site of the town's first swimming bath (now the rose garden, behind the Heritage Museum).

North of the railway close to the town centre, Norton Common had been retained in all the proposals for the design of the garden city, and is there to this day, partly tamed by the creation of the broad avenue along the line of the town's central axis, and partly developed with the tennis and bowls facilities, a children's play area and open air, heated swimming pool. Much of the area remains wild and rural, with the Pix brook meandering through it, a habitat for woodpeckers, bats, a colony of muntjac deer, and Letchworth's famous black squirrels.

The Greenway (www.greenway.org.uk) is a 13.6 mile trail through the green belt encircling the town, created by the Heritage Foundation to mark the town's centenary and providing an enjoyable facility for walkers, cyclists, riders and runners. Its creation was accompanied by the planting of many acres of woodland and the restoration of 1,095 yards of hedgerow. A grant of £250,000 was obtained from central government under its Countryside Management Scheme for environmentally friendly farming, which also includes the widening of field margins.

Small car parks are provided on the Greenway at three points – Radwell Meadows, Standalone Farm and Manor Wood, between Willian and Roxley Court. At Radwell there is a play and picnic area, with barbecues provided, Standalone Farm provides a café, and at Manor Wood there is a picnic area. Interpretative boards are provided at these points and also at Norton Pond, listing some of the plant, insect, bird, amphibian and mammal species that can be seen. Plant life is particularly rich in Radwell Meadows, both in the arable borders and meadows and along the infant River Ivel. The various aquatic in-

On the Greenway: 13.6 miles of path and track surrounding the Garden City with a range of places to visit en route.

Much of the Greenway, especially at the northern end, is close to water. There is a wide variety of bird life.

Carefully restored and maintained woodland and hedgerow attract many colourful creatures.

vertebrates, dragonflies, damsel flies and water boatmen, that enjoy the clear chalk stream support a number of higher species such as kingfishers and grey wagtails.

Near Manor Wood is Willian Arboretum, which contains 30 species of trees and shrubs.

Crossing the undulations formed by the headwaters of the chalk streams, the Greenway has no prolonged gradients yet offers fine views from its low summits. Those over the Bedfordshire plain from behind Highfield and from the Grange Estate are particularly bracing, as is the sight of the Weston hills from near the rugby club, while there is gentle rural scenery to be viewed all round the southern section. Wildlife is returning and the observant bird watcher will find, for example, skylarks, yellow hammers and partridges, all species that have struggled in the years of intensive farming. Even the sections of the walk close to the A1 motorway are not without interest, the hawthorn-laden banks being home to numerous rabbits and a hunting ground for kestrels.

A number of variations of Greenway walks is possible, thanks to the availability of permissive paths under the Countryside Stewardship Scheme. The Greenway website has maps showing some of the possibilities towards Radwell in the north east and around Roxley in the south.

Letchworth is crossed by route 12 of the **national cycle network**, from London to the north, which follows the line of the Greenway for part of its eastern section and is clearly signposted.

Long distance walkers should try the **Hertfordshire Way,** a series of linked paths going all round the county, which winds through Great Wymondley, Graveley and Weston. The **Icknield Way Path** extends from Icknield Way westwards from Wilbury Hills towards Ickleford, Pirton and Leagrave and east either to Norton Bury and Ashwell or via Baldock and then along the crest of the downs to Wallington, Sandon and Royston. At Wilbury Hill, there is a picnic area by the site of the iron age hill fort. Those setting off north should take the **Kingfisher Way,** which starts from Baldock but can be joined at Radwell. It meanders 20 miles for the length of the River Ivel, and a principal feature is the number of water mills, none of which is in use and most of which have been converted to residential or other uses, with the sole exception of Jordan's Mill south of Biggleswade, which is a major business complete with gift shop for passing tourists. At Henlow the path passes **Henlow Grange,** a 17th century house now a health farm. Trains can be caught back either from Arlesey (six miles) or Biggleswade (12 miles), though the finishing point at Tempsford (20 miles) is a notably public transport free zone and the best bet is to continue a further four miles along the Great Ouse Way to St Neots for a train home.

Wider circular walks from Letchworth might take you to Graveley or Weston in the south and east, or to Stotfold and Arlesey in the north. There is a particularly bracing walk from Willian south along the cycleway to Graveley, then from Graveley church by bridleway over the hill behind How Wood and either on to Weston or back to Letchworth Gate.

The little Pix brook, seen here at Norton, meanders through Letchworth.

The Wider Area

Letchworth is well located for a number of places to visit on day trips or half day trips. The nearby towns of **Baldock** and **Hitchin** are well supplied with pubs and restaurants and have some fine architecture, while **Stevenage** has a large shopping centre, a theatre, the **Gordon Craig**, and a modern leisure park with bowling, a multi-screen cinema, night clubs and American style diners. Perhaps inadvertently, the four North Herts towns of Baldock, Letchworth, Hitchin and Stevenage have grown to form one of Howard's projected "social cities" – a group of towns that collectively provide all the functions and amenities necessary for a full existence. They are even connected, as he described, by trains, which take a few minutes to make the inter-urban journey.

There are many attractive nearby villages. Perhaps worth especial mention are **Wallington**, high on the ridge and once the home of George Orwell, and **Ashwell** (www.ashwell.gov.uk), with many fine houses in its picturesque streets, an excellent village museum, and a massive church redolent of a wool trading past. The church is famous for its medieval graffiti whose unknown author laments the scourge brought by the Black Death. The springs at Ashwell form a source of the Cam and are home to a rare and ancient species of flatworm.

To the south **Welwyn Garden City,** Ebenezer Howard's second planned town, is an interesting contrast to Letchworth. It has a centre with a grand avenue and squares which is often considered more successful than Letchworth's, though the housing, while distinctive in its way, is less so. Nearby is the National Trust property of **Shaw's Corner,** down the sleepy lanes at Ayot St Lawrence, home of George Bernard Shaw, one of the early sponsors of the Garden City. He lived there from 1906 until his death in 1950, and the writer's early 20th century way of life, including the furnishings and memorabilia, is well represented.

To the north near Biggleswade is the **Shuttleworth Collection** of vintage aircraft, often with flying displays, together with a Swiss Garden. Heading east, beyond Royston, are **Wimpole Hall,** a National Trust property including a rare breeds farm and museum, little **Shepreth Zoo**, and the **Imperial War Museum** at Duxford Aerodrome, a major site with several hangars of exhibits and regular flying displays during the summer. All these are a 30-45 minutes drive, while Shepreth Zoo is adjacent to Shepreth station.

Slightly further away, **Cambridge**, with its ancient colleges, renowned museums, botanical gardens, and opportunities for punting on the river is within easy reach by coach, car or train.

Postscript

Lessons from Letchworth

Letchworth Garden City Heritage Foundation, successor to that original garden city company, names as one of its aims: 'To establish and promote the success of the Garden City "experiment" as a leading model for developing 21st century communities'. One of the ways in which it seeks to do this is by 'marketing the Garden City both nationally and internationally as a unique and successful community'.

In 2002, the Foundation hosted the conference of the International Planning History Society, and its leaders have also travelled to attend Garden City Conferences, such as in Kobe, Japan, in 2001.

What makes modern Letchworth different? It could be said that the Garden City movement has largely achieved its aims. Pleasant houses and gardens are everywhere across Britain – though the growing number of single person households means that a house and garden may no longer be the desirable end for many. As AA Gill, the writer (and former St Christopher School pupil), puts it – not necessarily complimentarily – in his book *The Angry Island – Hunting the English*:

> 'In trying peacefully and non-judgmentally to avoid the imminent smash and fracture and breakdown of his unfair society and to cure the sinful ills of the inner city and the bankruptcy of the country, he [Ebenezer Howard] saw and planned a future so prescient that no-one noticed he'd done it.'

Gill goes on to say:

> 'The cottages of Howard's original plan aren't monuments or totems of modern design like the Bauhaus house, because hardly anyone can live in a Bauhaus house, but Letchworth's cottages are everywhere.'

Town planning philosophy has changed since Howard's day; it is hard to imagine a private company buying and developing a new town site today given the constraints on planning and development that have been imposed by government, not least at the prompting of the Town and Country Planning Association, which was founded – as the Garden Cities Association – by Ebenezer Howard.

It could also be argued that many of the problems Howard was addressing have either vanished or changed dramatically. A major objective for Howard was to arrest the spread of the cities, particularly London. All, of course, have grown hugely since his time. It was only ever the London County Council, and then only in the special circumstances following the blitz, that showed any enthusiasm for relocating people – other cities were less than enthusiastic about assisting new town development in their areas. And although London is now ringed with new towns, any population they have absorbed has been insignificant compared with the growth of the national population. The impact of that growth in Letchworth and its neighbours is clearly seen in the map of Hitchin, Letchworth and Baldock in 1901 and 2001. Today's problem is not containing cities but containing urban sprawl in the face of this population pressure.

The 'unearned increment' concept has been appropriated by central government and would no longer be open for a single town to pursue. Health standards have risen hugely throughout the country, and clean air acts have removed the industrial pollution that was one of Howard's concerns.

Transport changes meanwhile mean that another of Howard's imperatives – that people should be able to walk or cycle to work – has far less force.

Letchworth's place as a pioneer in setting the standard for so much that is now taken for granted in creating a decent urban environment is unchallengeable. But is there anything today that still makes Letchworth special?

First, some of that early garden city spirit is still in evidence, in, for example, the wide range of groups, covering things as diverse as long distance walking, a thriving film society, an Irish language appreciation society and hosts of others, operating under the umbrella of the Arts and Leisure Group. It is there too in the huge range of adult education courses at the Settlement, and in the town's regular public debates on topical issues.

Second, the concept of 'town-country' is alive and well, especially since the creation of the Greenway footpaths encircling the town and the more general opening up of the green belt to residents.

Third, thanks to better design management by both the Heritage Foundation and the District Council, much new building in Letchworth is now returning to a deliberately vernacular style, with some good examples in Pixmore Way and at Creamery Court, at the Letchworth Gate entrance to the town.

Fourth, there remains the quasi-political message. Through its unique Heritage Foundation, Letchworth has retained much of the unearned increment principle. Most Letchworth houses nowadays are freehold, not leasehold with a rent payable to the garden city authority. But the Foundation has a healthy income from investments, business rents and farmland, and this is ploughed back into the town, with both major projects such as the refurbishment of the Broadway cinema or the creation of the Standalone Farm centre and a host of grants to local organisations, college students, and so on.

Finally, the town itself makes its own case. Now mature, its houses often hidden by shrubbery, it has its developed its own beauty, its own personality and its own uniqueness. It is a reference point for future generations of planners. By any yardstick, Letchworth must surely stand as a first-rate example of how to build a community.

Bibliography

Mervyn Miller, *Letchworth the First Garden City,* 1989, updated and revised 2002, Phillimore & Co Ltd., is the definitive history and analysis, scholarly and comprehensive. The 2002 edition benefits from more generous illustration.

Kenneth Johnson, *The Book of Letchworth,* Barracuda, 1976.
A very readable popular history by a local library assistant and newspaper columnist.

CB Purdom, *The Letchworth Achievement,* JM Dent & Sons, 1963.
Description by a pioneer of the battle to defend the principles of the Garden City in the 1960s.

Stanley Buder, *Visionaries and Planners,* Oxford University Press, 1990.
Critique by an American of the Garden City movement and its modern relevance, including continental and American comparisons.

Ebenezer Howard, *Tomorrow – A Peaceful Path to Real Reform,* 1898, republished with commentary 2003. The second edition, *Garden Cities of Tomorrow,* should be read as an abridged form of the original, lacking the final chapter and some drawings.

Colin Ward, *New Town, Home Town,* Calouste Gulbenkian Foundation, 1993.
An analysis of the principles of post war new town planning.

Helen Meller, *Towns, Plans and Society in Modern Britain,* Cambridge University Press, 1997, provides an analysis of British city and town development since the industrial revolution.

V W Miles, *The Cloisters, Letchworth 1907-1967,* the Lawrence Cloisters Trust 1967. A monograph on this unique building.

Keith Sell and Peter Cannell, *To The Glory of God,* published by North Avenue Methodist Church, 1994, relates the history of the Norton Mission and its connections with Gipsy Smith, whose biography is by David Lazell, *Gypsy From The Forest,* Bryntirion Press, 1997.

Reginald Snell, *St Christopher School 1915-1975*, details the origins and development of Letchworth's progressive school.

Philip Purser *The Last Great Tram Race and other Memoirs*, Hodder and Stoughton 1974, contains a delightfully wicked, and completely fictional, account of a celebration of what Purser describes as Ebenezer Day on Norton Common that develops into a bacchanalian orgy.

Useful websites

www.letchworth.com
www.letchworthgc.com
www.lgchf.com
www.north-herts.gov.uk
www.letchworthgardencity-council.org.uk
http://en.wikipedia.org/wiki/letchworth
www.letchworthgardencity.net
www.hertsheritage.org.uk
www.shopletchworth.com
www.davids-bookshops.co.uk
www.davids-music.co.uk

Index

INDEX